"*Disposable Americans* is as elo                        ve
copies to everyone you know.'
                              **Henry A.**                              ...olar
                                                        ...cMaster University

"In this brilliantly written, clearly articulated, and diligently documented book,
Paul Buchheit offers a practical real-world solution to our out-of-control
political/economic system. Read this book and share it far and wide!"
                    **Thom Hartmann**, author of *The Last Hours of Ancient Sunlight*

"In light of the presidential results of the 2016 election, Buchheit's exploration of
the increasing number of Americans who are economically disposable becomes a
vital read. This book enlightens readers into how so many people in the United
States have fallen into an financial crater."
                              **Mark Karlin**, Editor of BuzzFlash at *Truthout*

"In this beautifully-written, moving, and powerful book, Paul Buchheit
demonstrates convincingly that an out of control economy is destroying the lives
of most Americans. Fortunately, he also provides an antidote to the widening
misery and economic inequality that plague this nation, and shows how it can
be implemented."
                              **Lawrence S. Wittner**, Professor of History Emeritus,
                                                      University at Albany, SUNY

"Nearly half the people of the United States live in or perilously close to poverty.
Yet the bulk of our tax dollars go, directly or indirectly, to benefit America's most
affluent. In *Disposable Americans*, Paul Buchheit puts real faces on the numbers that
define our staggeringly unequal social order and gives us the information--and
inspiration—we need to forge a new and better future for us all."
                              **Sam Pizzigati**, co-editor of *Inequality.org* and
                                                  author of *The Rich Don't Always Win*

# DISPOSABLE AMERICANS

Inequality has dramatically increased in America, with few solutions on the horizon. Serious social inequalities persist. For example, the 14 richest Americans earned enough money from their investments in 2015 to hire two million preschool teachers (while the USA ranks low among developed countries in preschool enrollment). Following the Great Recession, the richest one percent took 116 percent of the new income gains, a statistic caused by so many middle-class Americans moving backward, many losing investments in property and experiencing interruptions in work. Author Paul Buchheit looks hopefully to solutions in a book that vividly portrays the rapidly changing inequality of American society. More Americans have become "disposable" as middle-class jobs have disappeared at an alarming rate. Buchheit presents innovative proposals that could quickly begin to reverse these trends, including a guaranteed basic income drawn from new revenues, such as a Financial Speculation Tax and a Carbon Tax. Discussing the challenges and obstacles to such measures, he finds optimism in past successes in American history.

Ideal for classroom assignment, the book uniquely pairs historical events with current, real-life struggles faced by citizens, pointing to measures that can improve personal and social well-being and trust in government.

**Paul Buchheit** taught economics at DePaul University and also has formal training in language development and cognitive science. He is the founder and developer of several social justice and educational websites (UsAgainstGreed.org, RappingHistory.org, YouDeserveFacts.org) and the editor of *American Wars: Illusions and Realities* (Clarity Press 2008).

## Critical Interventions: Politics, Culture, and the Promise of Democracy
*Edited by Henry A. Giroux, Susan Searls Giroux, and Kenneth J. Saltman*

# DISPOSABLE AMERICANS

## Extreme Capitalism and the Case for a Guaranteed Income

*Paul Buchheit*

Routledge
Taylor & Francis Group

NEW YORK AND LONDON

First published 2017
by Routledge
711 Third Avenue, New York, NY 10017

and by Routledge
2 Park Square, Milton Park, Abingdon, Oxon, OX14 4RN

*Routledge is an imprint of the Taylor & Francis Group, an informa business*

© 2017 Taylor & Francis

*Library of Congress Cataloging in Publication Data*
Names: Buchheit, Paul, author.
Title: Disposable Americans : extreme capitalism and the case for a
guaranteed income / Paul Buchheit.
Description: New York, NY : Routledge, 2017. | Series: Critical
interventions | Includes bibliographical references.
Identifiers: LCCN 2016044741| ISBN 9781138671751 (hardback) |
ISBN 9781138671768 (pbk.)
Subjects: LCSH: Guaranteed annual income--United States. | Income
distribution--United States. | Capitalism--United States. | Labor--
United States. | Working poor--United States. | United States--
Economic conditions--2009- | United States--Economic policy--2009-
Classification: LCC HC110.I5 B795 2017 | DDC 331.2/360973--dc23
LC record available at https://lccn.loc.gov/2016044741

ISBN: 978-1-138-67175-1 (hbk)
ISBN: 978-1-138-67176-8 (pbk)
ISBN: 978-1-315-61680-3 (ebk)

Typeset in Bembo and Stone Sans
by Saxon Graphics Ltd, Derby

# CONTENTS

# INTRODUCTION[1]

Our jobs are disappearing. In the not-too-distant future we might wait around for a package delivery, hurry off to class, grab a taxi downtown, consult with a financial advisor, meet the family for dinner, and then take the train home. All without being served by a single human being. No delivery person, no teacher, no cab driver, no financial advisor, no food server, no train conductor.

That may be disputed by free-market defenders, but even today many of our traditional mid-level jobs are being handled by fewer human beings as our workload is gradually surrendered to our own innovative technologies. The World Economic Forum says "we are on the cusp of a **Fourth Industrial Revolution** in which 'smart systems' in our homes, factories, farms, and entire cities will help get our work done."[2]

A variety of new jobs—and the dropping out of discouraged job-seekers—have padded the recent unemployment figures, but in large part today's work opportunities are lower wage and less secure forms of employment.[3] The jobs that made the middle class prosperous—manufacturing, education, construction, social services, customer service, transportation, administrative support—have dramatically declined since the recession.[4] Globalization is a big part of it. A *National Bureau of Economic Research* study found that the job loss from foreign import competition is ***not being replaced*** by jobs in other industries.[5]

Another major factor is the rapid rise of ***alternative work*** arrangements in the "1099 economy"—contract and "gig" jobs—which are impacting, according to a recent Harvard/Princeton study, "previously lagging sectors including transportation and warehousing, information and communications, education and health care, and public administration."[6]

For all the above reasons, traditional employer/employee relationships are fading away. High-level positions in engineering, project management, and finance are still in demand. But nine of the ten fastest growing occupations don't require a college degree.[7]

Yet our nation keeps making money. The 14 richest Americans made enough money from their investments in one year to hire two million preschool teachers, about four times the number of preschool teachers who currently have jobs in the United States.[8] Total U.S. wealth increased by a stunning 60 percent between 2009 and 2015, from $54 trillion to $86 trillion,[9] but three-quarters of that massive increase went to the richest ten percent of Americans.[10]

The health of Americans is tied to our nation's extreme inequality.[11] The lowest-income people live up to 15 years less than those at the high-income end.[12] As a result of their low pay and almost nonexistent savings, almost half of Americans would be **unable to afford a $400 emergency room visit** without borrowing money or selling personal items.[13] The resulting stress leads to mental and physical illness, and perhaps worse. The Centers for Disease Control reported a 24 percent increase in suicides in the first 15 years of this century.[14]

The correlations may not be entirely certain, but the evidence is accumulating. Our system of poorly regulated capitalism is causing destruction in American lives. As Thomas Piketty made clear in his book, *Capital in the 21st Century*, the growth of capital has outpaced that of productive labor, to the point that our economy is driven more and more by the creation of financial instruments rather than real goods. Hence, the redistribution of national wealth from preschoolers to billionaires.[15]

The chapters to follow will show the impact of extreme capitalism on children; on the poor and the sick and the elderly; on minorities; on women; on workers, especially young Americans; on soldiers; and on all average Americans, including the middle class and those just above and below, who make up approximately 90 percent of us, and who have become, as aptly expressed by Henry Giroux, increasingly **disposable** to the fortunate minority at the top of the wealth distribution.[16]

The disposability chapters together describe a process of **Americide**, the gradual killing off of the once-vibrant middle class of our society. The violence begins with economic oppression. But the resulting disparities in wealth and income have increasingly caused *physical* damage, both in the health of the American people and in the surge in violence in our poverty-stricken urban communities.

Each chapter on disposable Americans will begin with a story from the **PAST**, at a time when prospects may have seemed dim for a vulnerable class of people, yet were in reality teeming with hopefulness, as new technologies were beginning to create living-wage jobs, and as social dependencies were being strengthened in the waging or aftermath of war. Those moments from the past are in stark contrast to the **PRESENT** day, in which technology generates low-income jobs, while globalization allows multinational companies to seek the cheapest labor in all corners of the world. These rapidly occurring changes have been exacerbated by the rise of an economic system—starting in the era of Ayn Rand and Milton

Friedman and Reaganomics—based on individual gain, rather than on social interdependencies. And by the rise of a financial industry that has transformed the widespread fruits of productive labor into fees and interest and investment returns. The result has been *extreme and ever-worsening inequality*.

In an important sense, little has changed from past to present. Minorities and children and soldiers and workers and seniors are on one end. On the other is unimaginable wealth for relatively few people. Our nation started with dreams of equal opportunity. Then came deregulated capitalism. That brought opportunities for individuals who knew how to manipulate the markets, who had friends in high places, and who frequented the revolving door between business and politics. The wealth of John D. Rockefeller and Andrew Carnegie, and then Vanderbilt and Astor, was comparable to the modern fortunes of Bill Gates and Warren Buffett and the Waltons and the Kochs.[17] The inequality we see today has a long history.

Yet there is hope. Some of it will be seen in the **PERSONAL** stories that end the chapters. But that hopefulness, if it is to bear fruit, will require society to begin catching up to technology, to recognize the changing paradigm of human involvement in the nation's (and the world's) progress, and to reevaluate the meaning of "progress." All Americans, through their own effort and that of their ancestors, have contributed to the dramatically productive society that has compensated fewer and fewer people over time. Everyone deserves a *guaranteed living income*. How that is to be accomplished—in a way that appeals to Republicans and Democrats, liberals and neo-liberals, conservatives and progressives—is one of the objectives of the chapters to follow.

## What Exactly is a Guaranteed Income?

We need the assurance that every American family receives a sufficient living income as compensation for the great productivity and unprecedented levels of wealth derived from decades of new technologies funded by our tax dollars. We and our families have all contributed our labors and taxes over the past three-quarters of a century. But social equanimity lags far behind finance and technology, and thus the relatively few people positioned to exploit our new prosperity have reaped most of the benefits, in many cases under the pretense of achieving "self-made" fortunes. The truth is much different.

Our phones, our internet searches, our medications, our transportation systems, and our national security all originated with our tax dollars. Entrepreneurs certainly deserve compensation for their initiative and innovation, but for the most part the nation's accomplishments have arisen from the productive commons that is our heritage. A guaranteed income will only come about if 35 years of redistribution to the rich is reversed through the ideas and proposals to be presented in this book.

## Notes

1 www.DisposableAmericans.com/Credits (accessed November 14 2016).
2 "The Future of Jobs." The World Economic Forum, January 2016.
3 Kendzior, Sarah, "Why America's Impressive 5% Unemployment Rate Feels Like a Lie for So Many." *Quartz*, April 20, 2016.
4 "Regional Economic Press Briefing." New York Federal Reserve, May 21, 2014.
5 Autor, David H.; Dorn, David; and Hanson, Gordon H., "The China Shock: Learning from Labor Market Adjustment to Large Changes in Trade." National Bureau of Economic Research, January 2016.
6 Katz, Lawrence F. and Krueger, Alan B., "The Rise and Nature of Alternative Work Arrangements in the United States, 1995–2015." Harvard University, Princeton University, and NBER, March 29, 2016.
7 "Most New Jobs." Bureau of Labor Statistics, December 17, 2015.
8 Buchheit, Paul, "It Happened Again: How 14 People Made More Money Than the Entire Food Stamp Budget for 50,000,000 People." CommonDreams.org, October 6, 2014.
9 "Global Wealth Databook 2015." Credit Suisse, October 2015.
10 Personal Analysis (http://YouDeserveFacts.org/20151019_Analysis.txt), accessed October 19, 2015.
11 "Compilation of Research from 200 Studies on the Correlation between Financial Stress and Healthcare Costs." *Financial Finesse*, March 2011.
12 Chetty, Raj; Stepner, Michael; Abraham, Sarah; Lin, Shelby; Scuderi, Benjamin; Turner, Nicholas; Bergeron, Augustin; Cutler, David, "The Association Between Income and Life Expectancy in the United States, 2001–2014." *Journal of the American Medical Association*, April 10, 2016.
13 Gabler, Neal, "The Secret Shame of Middle-Class Americans." *The Atlantic*, May 2016; Morath, Eric, "Most Americans Don't Have Savings to Pay Unexpected Bill." *Wall Street Journal*, January 7, 2015.
14 Curtin, Sally C.; Warner, Margaret; Hedegaard, Holly, "Suicide Rates for Females and Males by Race and Ethnicity: United States, 1999 and 2014." National Center for Health Statistics, Centers for Disease Control, April 2016.
15 Piketty, Thomas, *Capital in the Twenty-First Century*. Harvard University Press, 2014.
16 Giroux, Henry, *Disposable Youth, Racialized Memories, and the Culture of Cruelty*. Routledge, 2012.
17 Housel, Morgan, "Who Will Be the World's First Trillionaire?" *USA Today*, October 24, 2013; "Inside The 2015 Forbes 400." Forbes (www.forbes.com/sites/luisakroll/2015/09/29/inside-the-2015-forbes-400-facts-and-figures-about-americas-wealthiest/#523665dd28f8), accessed September 29, 2015.

## Bibliography

Acemoglu, Daron and Robinson, James, *Why Nations Fail: The Origins of Power, Prosperity, and Poverty*. Crown, 2013.
Collins, Chuck, *99 to 1: How Wealth Inequality is Wrecking the World and What We Can Do About It*. Berrett-Koehler, 2013.

Evans, Brad and Giroux, Henry A., *Disposable Futures: The Seduction of Violence in the Age of the Spectacle*. City Lights, 2015.

Giroux, Henry. *Disposable Youth, Racialized Memories, and the Culture of Cruelty*. Routledge, 2012.

Giroux, Henry, *America at War with Itself*. City Lights Open Media, 2016.

Hedges, Chris, *Empire of Illusion: The End of Literacy and the Triumph of Spectacle*. Nation Books, 2010.

Hedges, Chris, *Wages of Rebellion*. Brilliance Audio MP3, 2015.

Johnston, David Cay, Editor, *Divided: The Perils of Our Growing Inequality*. The New Press, 2014.

Pinkow, Linda and Pizzigati, Sam, *Dollars & Sense Collective, The Wealth Inequality Reader (4th Edition)*. Economic Affairs Bureau, 2013.

Pizzigati, Sam, *Greed and Good: Understanding and Overcoming the Inequality that Limits Our Lives*. Rowman & Littlefield, 2004.

Reich, Robert, *Saving Capitalism: For the Many, Not the Few*. Knopf, 2015.

Smith, Hedrick, *Who Stole the American Dream?* Random House, 2012.

Stiglitz, Joseph, *The Price of Inequality: How Today's Divided Society Endangers Our Future*. W.W. Norton, 2012.

Taibbi, Matt, *The Divide: American Justice in the Age of the Wealth Gap*. Spiegel & Grau, 2014.

Wolff, Richard D., *Capitalism Hits the Fan: The Global Economic Meltdown and What to Do About It*. Olive Branch Press, 2013.

Yates, Michael D., *The Great Inequality*. Routledge, 2016.

# 1

# WORKERS

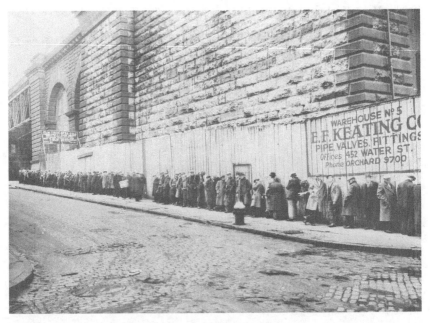

**FIGURE 1.1** New York, NY. Bread line beside the Brooklyn Bridge approach.
Library of Congress (www.loc.gov/pictures/item/owi2001046116/PP/).

## The Past: Downtrodden Laborers[1]

Starting in the 1840s, at the time of the potato famine in Ireland, a half-million Irish immigrants arrived in America almost penniless, packed into sailing ships under the most vile conditions. Said one witness:

Who can imagine the horrors of even the shortest passage in an emigrant ship crowded beyond its utmost capacity of stowage with unhappy beings of all ages, with fever raging in their midst...one-fourth, or one-third, or one-half of the entire number in different stages of the disease; many dying, some dead; the fatal poison intensified by the indescribable foulness of the air breathed and rebreathed by the gasping sufferers—the wails of children, the ravings of the delirious.[2]

There was little improvement upon arrival, as many thousands were herded into freight cars to Pennsylvania mines to replace English-speaking workers at a much lower wage. Exploitation by business owners, along with the resentment of displaced workers, made life almost unbearable for the immigrants and their families. Few safety measures were taken by management. Thousands of mine workers, about a quarter of them children, faced constant danger like the loss of hands or feet or fingers, collapsing walls, or bodies crushed by rail cars. An 1869 fire at the Avondale Mine took the lives of 110 coal miners; the company had rejected the expense of a secondary exit.

## Lowell Girls[3]

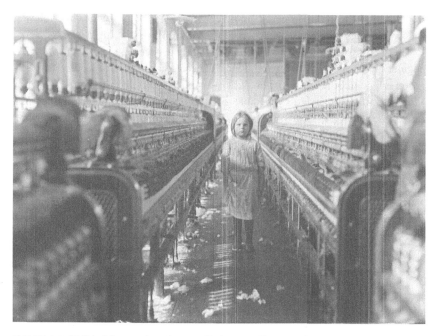

**FIGURE 1.2** Child laborer in the Mollohan Mills, Newberry, South Carolina, December 1908.
National Child Labor Committee collection at the Library of Congress (https://commons.wikimedia.org/wiki/File:Child_laborer.jpg).

In the late 1800s, young women worked in the cotton textile mills of Lowell, Massachusetts from 5 a.m. until 7 p.m. in airless rooms filled with dust particles and the clattering, staccato noises of hundreds of milling machines. Along with the oppressive conditions, girls as young as 13 were constantly the targets of sexual abuse by managers, to the extent that women employed by the mills were assumed to be tainted and unfit for marriage into respectable families. Many were to remain unwanted "spinsters."

Activist Harriet Hanson Robinson, who started out as an eleven-year-old mill worker, later described the plight of the Lowell Girl: "In the eyes of her overseer she was but a brute, a slave, to be beaten, pinched and pushed about. It was to overcome this prejudice that such high wages had been offered to women that they might be induced to become millgirls, in spite of the opprobrium that still clung to this degrading occupation." In 1836, hundreds of workers organized a "turn-out" to protest wage cuts and rent hikes. It was one of the first strikes in U.S. history.

## Pullman Violence[4]

On May 11, 1894 four thousand factory workers at the Pullman Company near Chicago went out on strike. The uncompromising George Pullman had responded to the 1893–4 depression by cutting wages 30 percent, while refusing to lower rents in the houses that were leased to most of his employees.

The "company town" of George Pullman had been an experiment in social engineering—or social control. Workers were leased modern houses in well-groomed neighborhoods that included a church and library. Bars were not allowed. Pullman managers were able to gain entry into rental units to inspect the interiors, and even to demand changes. The arrangement began to fall apart when the workers couldn't meet their rental payments. Said one resident: "I have seen men with families of eight or nine children crying because they got only three or four cents after paying their rent."

To counter the strike, Pullman hired replacement workers, including blacks, a decision that added racial tension to the already volatile mix of anger and vengeance-seeking. He had the business-friendly media on his side, helping to convince the public that the strikers were greedy immigrants and anti-American anarchists. But Pullman ultimately lost his battle in the Illinois Supreme Court. When he passed away soon after at the age of 66, his casket at Graceland Cemetery was surrounded by several feet of concrete embedded with steel rails, to ensure that former employees wouldn't desecrate his burial site.

## Demanding a 76-Hour Work Week

**FIGURE 1.3** Brooklyn barbers' strike of 1913, Union Square, New York City.
George Grantham Bain collection at the Library of Congress (https://commons.wikimedia.org/wiki/File:Ettor-JJ-barbersstrike-nyc-130517.jpg).

A reader may have to look twice at the photograph to believe the numbers. Barbers were demanding a shorter work day—down to 12 hours, and 16 on Saturday. The police, too, were like other workers of the time. In 1919, police officers worked over 80 hours a week and were paid about 25 cents per hour (about $3.25 today). Over two-thirds of the 1,500 Boston police officers went on strike. As the city was looted, the *Wall Street Journal* wailed, "Lenin and Trotsky are on their way."

## The Horrors of Factory Work for Women[5]

How would you like to iron a shirt a minute? Think of standing at a mangle just above the washroom with the hot steam pouring up through the floor for 10, 12, 14 and sometimes 17 hours a day! Sometimes the floors are made of cement and then it seems as though one were standing on hot coals, and the workers are dripping with perspiration...They are...breathing air laden with particles of soda, ammonia, and other chemicals.

**FIGURE 1.4** Image of Triangle Shirtwaist Factory fire on March 25, 1911.
First published on front page of *The New York World* on March 26, 1911 (https://commons.
wikimedia.org/wiki/File:Image_of_Triangle_Shirtwaist_Factory_fire_on_March_25_-_1911.jpg).

**FIGURE 1.5** Bodies from Triangle Shirtwaist Factory fire, March 1911.
Bain Collection, Library of Congress (www.loc.gov/pictures/item/98502780/).

On March 25, 1911, at the Triangle Shirtwaist Factory in New York City, 146 garment workers died in a fire, most of them young immigrant women, some as young as 14. They toiled from nine to fourteen hours a day, six days a week, cramped together in little work spaces, forced to keep up a pace of 50 stitches per second in the preparation of blouses, all for 15 cents an hour. They were all on the eighth and ninth floors when the fire started near the end of the Saturday work shift. Up on the tenth floor were Max Blanck and Isaac Harris, the "Shirtwaist Kings."

The factory was not equipped for safety. There were few government regulations in the early 1900s. Blanck and Harris had weathered a massive strike by garment workers in 1909, led by activist Clara Lemlich, who along with her unlikely partner Ann Morgan, daughter of financier J.P. Morgan, orchestrated the largest walkout in New York City's history. Safety in the factory was one of the issues. Despite harassment and beatings by the police (who were paid off by Blanck and Harris), the garment workers finally won some wage concessions, although they were unable to form a union.

The fire was apparently started by a cigarette butt in an old fabric waste bin. Only two exits existed: one quickly became blocked by smoke and flames, and the other was locked; the only man with a key ran off at the first hint of fire. A few workers hurried down the smoke-filled stairway to the eighth floor, only to be trapped between the locked door and the flames above them. Blanck and Harris had escaped to the roof, without alerting the ninth floor.

In the final minutes, as the elevator made its final descent, the few fortunate women inside heard the impact of bodies falling on the elevator roof. About 20 girls ran out to an incomplete, poorly constructed fire escape, which collapsed under their weight, hurling them all one hundred feet to the sidewalk. A reporter wrote, "I learned a new sound that day, a sound more horrible than description can picture—the thud of a speeding living body on a stone sidewalk."

Everyone else was trapped inside. The fire ladders only reached the sixth floor. Eyewitnesses described the scene: "Horrified and helpless, the crowds—I among them—looked up at the burning building, saw girl after girl appear at the reddened windows, pause for a terrified moment, and then leap to the pavement below...This went on for what seemed a ghastly eternity." At some of the windows, girls engulfed by flames joined in an embrace before leaping to their deaths. Fire nets were ripped open by the fast-falling bodies. In the words of a reporter, one girl who was "screaming with clothes and hair ablaze, plunged like a living torch to the street."

Later, some of the same police who had beaten the young strikers a year earlier now quietly lifted their lifeless bodies from the street.

Blanck and Harris were acquitted of all charges of manslaughter for blocking escape routes and ignoring simple safety measures. They took their insurance money and faded into obscurity.

### Ludlow Massacre[6]

The Ludlow Massacre of April 20, 1914 was an attack by the National Guard and mining company guards on a tent colony of over a thousand striking coal miners and their families in Ludlow, Colorado. The strike, which had started seven months earlier, was organized by the United Mine Workers to protest low pay, dangerous working conditions, and corporate control over the workers' lives. They were up against a prominent owner, John D. Rockefeller, Jr. Two weeks before the massacre, Rockefeller had told a Congressional committee, "These men have not expressed any dissatisfaction with their conditions. The records show that the conditions have been admirable...A strike has been imposed upon the company from the outside." His hatred for the union had driven him to extreme measures. Workers had initially been evicted from company-owned shacks, and when that failed to end the strike, management hired gunmen to attack the tent colony. Several miners had been killed in the first few months of the strike. Now, in April of 1914, the governor of Colorado allowed Rockefeller to pay for the privilege of using the National Guard to fight the striking miners.

On April 20, guardsmen made the tragic decision to set fire to the tent camp. Most of the residents ran for the nearby hills, with bullets screaming past them. Not until the next day was it learned that pits had been dug to shelter women and children, and that 12 of them had been trapped underground, to suffocate or burn in the inferno. *The New York Times* reported, "The Ludlow camp is a mass of charred debris, and buried beneath it is a story of horror imparalleled in the history of industrial warfare. In the holes which had been dug for their protection against the rifles' fire the women and children died like trapped rats when the flames swept over them."

Rockefeller denied responsibility: "There was no Ludlow massacre. The engagement started as a desperate fight for life by two small squads of militia against the entire tent colony...While this loss of life is profoundly to be regretted, it is unjust in the extreme to lay it at the door of the defenders of law and property."

In retaliation for the slaughter, miners went on a rampage over the following week, destroying company property and continuing the shootouts with the National Guard. Despite the length and intensity of the walkout, few changes were made in wages or working conditions. Anywhere from 60 to 200 men, women, and children died during the 15-month strike. Not a single individual on the side of management was charged with a crime. Today, Ludlow is a ghost town.

## Workers in the Present Day

### Demanding Self-Reliance of People Who Can't Find a Living-Wage Job[7]

The Koch-funded Heritage Foundation proclaimed, "Helping the poor should mean promoting individual freedom through self-reliance."[8] The Cato Institute chimed in: "SNAP helps breed dependency and undermines the work ethic."[9]

Nearly two-thirds of all working-age poor are actually working,[10] but unable to earn a living wage, forcing them to rely on food stamps, which only provide about $5 a day per person for meals.[11] In addition, over 83 percent of all benefits going to low-income people are for the elderly, the disabled, or working households.

Much of Congress vilifies the poor for laziness while doing little to provide employment opportunities. In 2011, Senate Republicans **killed a proposed $447 billion jobs bill** that would have added about two million jobs to the economy. Congressional members filibustered Nancy Pelosi's "Prevention of Outsourcing Act," even as a million jobs were being outsourced,[12] and they temporarily blocked the "Small Business Jobs Act." In April, 2013 only one member of Congress **bothered to show up** for a hearing on unemployment.[13] When asked what he would do to bring jobs to Kentucky, Mitch McConnell responded, "That is not my job. It is the primary responsibility of the state Commerce Cabinet."[14]

### Some Numbers for the "Entitlement" Bashers[15]

Americans constantly hear about the threat of "entitlements," which in the case of Social Security and Medicare are more properly defined as "earned benefits." The real threat is the array of entitlements demanded by the very rich. Recent **annual** numbers may help to put our country's expenses and benefits in perspective.

### $220 Billion: Teacher Salaries

According to the Bureau of Labor Statistics, there are just over four million preschool, primary, secondary, and special education school teachers in the U.S., earning an average of $54,740.[16] It's a frightening commentary on our value system that the total income of over a third of a million preschool teachers is less than the combined income of just five big-money speculators.[17]

### $246 Billion: State and Local Pensions

Census data show a total annual (2012) payout of about $246 billion.[18] Only about two-fifths of this came from state and local governments, with the remainder funded by employee contributions and investment earnings. A 2010 Pew study showed a little over $100 billion in annual state contributions to pensions, health care, and non-pension benefits.[19] A study by Good Jobs First found that in just ten states, "the total annual cost of corporate subsidies, tax breaks and loopholes exceeds the total current annual pension costs."[20]

## $398 Billion: Safety Net

The 2013 safety net (non-medical) included the Supplemental Nutrition Assistance Program (SNAP), WIC (Women, Infants, Children), Child Nutrition, Earned Income Tax Credit, Supplemental Security Income, Temporary Assistance for Needy Families, Education and Training, and Housing.[21]

## $863 Billion: Social Security

Social Security is the major source of income for most of the elderly, and it is an earned benefit. As of 2010, according to the Urban Institute, the average two-earner couple making average wages throughout their lifetimes receive less in Social Security benefits than they paid in.[22]

## $2,200 Billion: Tax Avoidance

That's $2.2 trillion in tax expenditures, tax underpayments, tax havens, and corporate nonpayment. It is estimated that two-thirds of tax breaks accrue to the top quintile of taxpayers.[23]

## $5,000 Billion: Investment Wealth

That's $5 trillion dollars a year, the annual amount gained in U.S. wealth from the end of 2008 to the middle of 2013. Even though the whole country continued to grow in productivity, most of the new wealth went to the very richest people. According to Oxfam, the wealthiest one percent captured 95 percent of post-financial crisis growth since 2009, while the bottom 90 percent became poorer.[24]

## Five Reasons Why Cutting Social Security Would Be Irrational[25]

Even for Congress. They, and others who apparently don't study the facts, believe that Social Security is a government handout. But "entitlement" means that people who have paid into a program all their lives are entitled to a reasonable return on their investment. A better definition, as pointed out by Mark Karlin, is a "mandated retirement savings plan."[26]

Cutting this popular and well-run and life-sustaining program would be irrational. There are many reasons for this.

## 1. Americans Have Paid for It Throughout their Working Lives

As noted above, the average two-earner couple making average wages throughout their lifetimes receive less in Social Security benefits than they paid in. Same for single males. Same by now for single females. One-earner couples get back more than they paid in.[27]

## 2. It's a Small Benefit, but Most Seniors Depend on It

The average Social Security benefit is less than $15,000 a year, but most of our seniors rely on this for the majority of their income. Even the second-richest quartile of Americans depends on Social Security for over half of its retirement income.

## 3. It's Been Well-Run for Over Half a Century

The poverty rate has decreased dramatically over the past 50 years, in large part because of the benefits of the Social Security program.

Social Security is running on a surplus of $2.6 trillion, it's funded until 2037, it cannot run out of money, it cannot contribute to the deficit, it has lower administrative costs than private sector 401k retirement plans, and it's wildly popular.

On top of all this, a report by the AARP Public Policy Institute found that Social Security stimulates the economy, adding more than $1 trillion to the U.S. economy each year as recipients spend their benefits on goods and services.[28]

Dean Baker calls Social Security "perhaps the greatest success story of any program in US history."

## 4. The Free-Market Alternative Doesn't Work for Most Americans

The free-market alternative is ***everybody for themselves***. That's fine for people with good jobs and retirement plans. But stunningly, the number of private sector workers covered by a pension with a guaranteed payout has dropped from 60 percent to 10 percent in a little over 30 years.

Americans are going into debt faster than they're saving for retirement, and those able to put something aside often make the wrong choices with their money.

Financial experts, who generally speak for the people with enough money to hire a financial expert, tell us to have $200,000 to $300,000 in personal retirement savings. Most Americans have about a tenth of that, less than $25,000.[29]

## 5. Redistribution Has Moved Retirement Money from the Middle Class to the Rich

Tax Expenditures—subsidies from special deductions, exemptions, exclusions, credits, capital gains, and loopholes that move tax money to the richest taxpayers—are estimated to be worth up to eight percent of GDP, or about $1.2 trillion.[30]

That alone is more than enough to pay for Social Security ($883 billion).

Because of this misdirected revenue, government has been forced to borrow from Social Security to fund its programs.[31] Most notably, George W. Bush took public retirement money to pay for his two wars and his tax cuts for the rich.

## Personal Stories of the Underemployed[32]

To see her, to meet her, or to view her impressive resumé, you would never guess this highly accomplished professional is part of the 62 percent of Americans with no emergency savings. You would also never guess that she has been living on food stamps, and that she has received Medicaid for several years. In fact, she's been living under the kind of extreme emotional duress and stress which comes from living month-to-month, with the ever-present concern of meeting essential expenses. This from a person who, for years, always paid her bills on time and was never accustomed to relying on government assistance. That has a way of driving one's self-esteem to the floor.

Due to her economic circumstances, and because she is single and without a family, she is living in a remote, rural county near the greater San Francisco Bay area, where rents are cheap. The downside is that she is living in the poorest county in California. Neighbors include drug users and dealers, members of gangs, and people with a plethora of unhealthy and uncivil behaviors. She resides in a tiny, three-room brick house with no insulation or heat, with the exception of two plug-in heat fans, which she turns on judiciously (along with the burners of the stove when it gets really cold). Any travel to jobs, business networking, or "normal" civilization is an hour-and-a-half away. Rent, two unexpected car breakdowns, basic living expenses, and auto-maintenance costs have consumed all her earnings from occasional part-time jobs.

How does this happen to someone with almost 40 years in a successful business career, with 20 years of experience running a business, and almost 30 years in marketing and sales, at the top of every sales team of which she has been a part, and with a history of selling multi-million-dollar deals? In 2008, the economic crash took her business of 20 years to levels she had never seen before. Within a couple of years, the small company had failed. Depression followed, and she was forced into poverty, having to move from an idyllic wine country town to the impoverished and litter-ridden town in which she now lives. As such, she began a side career doing part-time low-wage jobs, including catering and wine-tasting services, medical-marijuana trimming, and anything necessary—short of prostitution.

Since the crash of 2008, her expectations have been reduced to junior and mid-level job opportunities. She's tired of hearing from headhunters and prospective employers how "impressive" her resumé is. During these years of economic challenge, she has had to ask friends for money, a highly embarrassing and soul-wounding necessity, with all the stigma of beggary weighing on her once-independent being. As a result, she's watched friends drop from her life, and the personal loss is almost too much to bear. She recalls, with reluctance, one of her worst evenings, when she searched online for "painless ways to commit suicide."

An instructor at Chicago's City Colleges recalls boarding a north suburban bus one winter afternoon and seeing one of his students, Reggie M., backpack at his side, resting his head on the window. He straightened up at the sight of his former teacher, inviting him to sit down.

"Do you live up this way, Reggie?"

"No, I live on the south side. I just got off work, heading down to school."

School was a bus and a train away, about an hour's ride. Another train would take him to the south side after school.

"I work 7 to 3, take evening classes now."

"So you come that far every morning at 7 o'clock?"

"Yeah, I leave at 5:30. Not bad, I can study on the train. The problem is that I only see my kid for an hour at 9 p.m., if he's not in bed."

The oppressiveness of the schedule was readily apparent to the teacher, who was impressed by Reggie's apparently easygoing acceptance of his current situation. Some further conversation revealed that he worked at a suburban food court, at a pay scale that remained private, although likely just over minimum wage. His wife was looking for a job, although that depended on childcare arrangements.

The college instructor didn't see Reggie after that. But he often thought about his former student.

Rick lives in a small town in southwest Michigan. He's a carpenter, an electrician, a plumber, an auto mechanic, a machinist, a home designer and builder, and a contracting supervisor. But he's unemployed.

He's the first to admit that he could be trying harder to find work, at least part-time. He still gets up on the roof to lay shingles. But at the age of 59, and partially disabled from his last full-time job about ten years ago, he looks for projects that allow him to supervise the area's plentiful supply of underemployed young men. Rick's a "good ol' boy," with plenty of friends who've collaborated with him in the past. But, he says, "everyone's struggling…too much competition out there."

With $200 a month in government support, food stamps, and occasional odd jobs, he gets by. He built his own well-insulated little house a few years ago, and he drives an old pickup that was scheduled for a few snowplowing jobs until the transmission gave out. His former factory employer almost exclusively hires day laborers. His former summer jobs in the southwest Michigan blueberry fields have been taken over by families of migrant workers who, according to Rick, are paid less than minimum wage. Even after ten years, his disability claim hasn't been approved. So Rick sits in his driveway with his dog, enjoying the peacefulness of the woods adjoining his property, welcoming an occasional neighbor, drinking some wine when he can afford it, and waiting for return calls on job prospects that rarely seem to come his way.

## Notes

1  Zinn, Howard, *A People's History of the United States* (Chapter 10). Harper Press, 2005.
2  *The Handbook of the Women's Trade Union Industrial League* quoted in Howard Zinn, op. cit.
3  Robinson, Harriet H., "Early Factory Labor in New England," in *Massachusetts Bureau of Statistics of Labor, Fourteenth Annual Report*. Boston: Wright & Potter, 1883; "Lowell Mill Girls." *Wikipedia.com.*
4  "People & Events: George Pullman (1831–1897)." *American Experience*, Public Broadcasting System.
5  "Triangle Fire." *American Experience*, Public Broadcasting System; "Triangle Shirtwaist Fire in New York City." *This Day in History*, March 25, 1911.
6  "Militia Slaughters Strikers at Ludlow, Colorado." *This Day in History*, April 20, 1914; Mauk, Ben, "The Ludlow Massacre Still Matters." *The New Yorker*, April 18, 2014.
7  Buchheit, Paul, "Five Great American Hypocrisies." NationOfChange.org, October 12, 2015.
8  Sheffield, Rachel, "Food Stamp Participation the Highest Ever…and Growing." *Daily Signal*, April 23, 2012.
9  Tanner, Michael D., "SNAP Theatrics Fall Flat." CATO Institute, from *National Review*, June 26, 2013.
10  Gould, Elise, "Poor People Work: A Majority of Poor People Who Can Work Do." Economic Policy Institute, May 19, 2015.
11  "USDA Budget Summary." U.S. Dept. of Agriculture, 2015.
12  Wessel, David, "U.S. Firms Keen to Add Foreign Jobs." *Wall Street Journal*, November 22, 2011.
13  "Lawmaker Unemployment Hearing Attended by Single Member of Congress at Opening." *Huffington Post*, April 24, 2013.
14  Lewison, Jed, "Mitch McConnell says bringing jobs to Kentucky 'is not my job.'" *Daily Kos*, Apr 25, 2014.
15  Buchheit, Paul, "Some Numbers for the 'Entitlement' Bashers." NationOfChange. org, August 25, 2014.
16  "Occupational Employment Statistics." Bureau of Labor Statistics.
17  Taub, Stephen, "The Rich List: The Highest-Earning Hedge Fund." *Institutional Investor's Alpha*, May 6, 2014.
18  "2014 Survey of Public Pensions: State & Local Data." U.S. Census Bureau.
19  "The Trillion Dollar Gap." The Pew Center on the States, February 2010.

20  "Putting State Pension Costs in Context: How They Compare to the Cost of Corporate Subsidies, Tax Breaks and Loopholes." Good Jobs First, January 2014.

21  "Policy Basics: Where Do Our Federal Tax Dollars Go?" Center on Budget and Policy Priorities, updated March 4, 2016.

22  Steuerle, C. Eugene and Quakenbush, Caleb, "Social Security and Medicare Taxes and Benefits over a Lifetime." Urban Institute, 2012.

23  "Who Gains Most from Tax Breaks?" *New York Times*, April 13, 2012.

24  "Working for the Few." Oxfam, January 20, 2014.

25  Buchheit, Paul, "Five Reasons Why Cutting Social Security Would Be Irrational." Alternet.org, October 27, 2013.

26  Karlin, Mark, "Social Security Pumps $2 Into US Economy for Every Benefit Dollar Spent." *Truthout Buzzflash*, October 22, 2013.

27  Steuerle, C. Eugene and Quakenbush, Caleb, op. cit.

28  Koenig, Gary and Myles, Al, "Social Security's Impact on the National Economy." *AARP*, September 2013.

29  "EBRI's 2013 Retirement Confidence Survey: Perceived Savings Needs Outpace Reality for Many." Employee Benefit Research Institute, March 2013.

30  Rogers, Allison and Toder, Eric, "Trends in Tax Expenditures, 1985–2016." Urban-Brookings Tax Policy Center, September 16, 2011.

31  Ohlemacher, Stephen, "Fact Check: Social Security Adds to Budget Deficit." Yahoo! Finance, August 13, 2012.

32  Personal Interviews.

## Bibliography

Alstott, Anne L., *A New Deal for Old Age: Toward a Progressive Retirement*. Harvard University Press, 2016.

Altman, Nancy and Kingson, Eric, *Social Security Works! Why Social Security Isn't Going Broke and How Expanding It Will Help Us All*. The New Press, 2015.

Bly, David, *We All Do Better*. Itasca Books, 2016.

Cohen, Adam, *Nothing to Fear: FDR's Inner Circle and the Hundred Days that Created Modern America*. Penguin Books, 2010.

Ehrenreich, Barbara, *Nickel and Dimed: On (Not) Getting by in America*. Picador, 2011.

Hartmann, Thom, *Screwed: The Undeclared War Against the Middle Class—And What We Can Do about It*. Berrett-Koehler, 2007.

Hill, Steven, *Expand Social Security Now!: How to Ensure Americans Get the Retirement They Deserve*. Beacon Press, 2016.

Huws, Ursula, *Labor in the Global Digital Economy*. Monthly Review Press, 2015.

Zinn, Howard, *A People's History of the United States*. Harper Press, 2005.

# 2

# WHY WE NEED A GUARANTEED INCOME. SOON.

> Amy and I emailed back and forth to find an available time slot. She was efficient and gracious, considerate of my schedule constraints, and so polite in her responses that, with the meeting arranged, I began typing up a brief thank-you. Then I glanced at her email signature…"powered by artificial intelligence."
>
> Carolyn O'Hara, Managing Editor, *The Week*, November 13, 2015

American jobs are being eliminated. Many that remain are being downsized. The benefits of a half-century of productivity, in which we and our parents and grandparents all played a role, have largely accrued to the relatively few people who know how to make money by coordinating all the technological components, or by managing the money that derives from American innovation.

It might be argued that we've been here before, that similar concerns about the takeover of technology surfaced during the Second Industrial Revolution and the Space Race.[1] Economist Dean Baker scoffs: "Large numbers of elite thinkers are running around terrified that we will have millions of people who have no work because the robots have eliminated the need for their labor…The remarkable aspect to the robot story is that it is actually a very old story. We have been seeing workers displaced by technology for centuries, this is what productivity growth is." *The Atlantic* concurs: "The job market defied doomsayers in those earlier times, and according to the most frequently reported jobs numbers, it has so far done the same in our own time." The fear of job loss is called the "Luddite Fallacy" after the early nineteenth-century British textile workers who smashed the new weaving machines that threatened their jobs.

But there are *two clear differences* now: (1) In the past, technology created manufacturing jobs, white-collar jobs, HIGHER-PAYING jobs. Now, the only one of the ten fastest-growing occupations that pays over $33,000 per year is nursing.[2] And (2) Globalization has outsourced middle-income jobs, such as those in manufacturing, which is still dropping after the 2009 recession.[3] Because of globalization, jobs are being outsourced, not only from rich to poor countries, but also from one developing nation to another, as, for example, from China to Vietnam.[4]

And there is *a third reason*, less apparent, but perhaps more critical to the long-term paradigm change in the evolution of the labor force. Noam Chomsky, whose early work in linguistics paved the way for natural language processing by machine, said, "If [technology is] used to free up the workforce for more creative work…then it's for the good."[5] But identifying this creative work is the challenge for humanity. The intensely creative work powering today's intelligent machinery is being done by fewer and fewer people. The evolution of artificial intelligence is vastly outpacing the ability of human beings to equitably benefit from the phenomenon to which they've all contributed.

New research is beginning to confirm the permanent nature of job loss. Based on analysis that one reviewer calls "some of the most important work done by economists in the last twenty years," a National Bureau of Economic Research study found that national employment levels have fallen in U.S. industries that are vulnerable to import competition, *without offsetting job gains in other industries*.[6] In *The Rise and Fall of American Growth*, economist Robert J. Gordon casts doubt on our nation's ability to recreate its rapid economic growth from 1870 to 1970, although he blames a declining level of productivity in information technology.[7] Either way, jobs are being downsized or eliminated. Bloomberg columnist Megan McArdle summarizes, "Historically, the U.S. economy had done a pretty good job of reabsorbing displaced labor. Recent evidence has shown that to be less true than in the past."[8]

## The Disappearing Job

The elimination of middle-class American jobs started before the 1990s tech boom, as Louis Uchitelle documents in his 2006 book, *The Disposable American*.[9] The deregulation of industries in the 1970s and 1980s, and the layoffs caused by outsourcing in the 1990s, particularly as accelerated by Bill Clinton's free trade policies, all contributed to the phenomenon of the expendable American worker. Authors Charles Derber and Yale Magrass call that worker "The Surplus American," one of the increasingly redundant 99 percent of our nation.[10]

*The Wall Street Journal*, reporting on a Georgetown University study, concludes that "many middle-wage occupations, those with average earnings between $32,000 and $53,000, have collapsed."[11] *Collapsed*. High-wage occupations in technology, medicine, science, engineering, and finance are still plentiful, and so are low-wage occupations in food service, retail, and personal care. But middle-income positions are fading away.

A more recent Harvard/Princeton study goes even further, concluding that the increase in *alternative work* arrangements—contract and "gig" jobs—is impacting previously stable sectors such as manufacturing, transportation, information technology, education, health care, and public administration.[12] Contract work is even invading the low-income ranks, making them even lower-income, as in Silicon Valley, where tech experts are increasingly being served by janitors, bus drivers, food service workers, and security guards who are no longer employees with benefits, and who make only about 70 percent of the salaries of hired employees.[13]

The evidence for the diminishing job keeps accumulating. A U.S. Mayors study found that "recovery" jobs pay 23 percent less than the jobs they replaced.[14] The National Employment Law Project estimates that low-wage jobs accounted for 22 percent of job losses, but 44 percent of subsequent job gains.[15] *Business Insider, Huffington Post*, and *The Wall Street Journal* all concur: the unemployment rate is remaining low because of low-paying jobs.[16]

Today's tech and telecom companies build products that require fewer American workers, fewer middle-income workers, and fewer workers overall. But more big-salary workers. Netflix, for example, serves 57 million customers with fewer than 2,200 employees, who have a median salary of $180,000.[17] As noted in *The Atlantic*,[18] 50 years ago AT&T was worth $267 billion in today's dollars and employed about 750,000 workers. Today, Google is worth $370 billion, but employs only about 55,000 workers. Robert Reich notes that much of the photo processing once done by Kodak with 145,000 employees is now done by Instagram with 13 employees. Facebook's messaging application, WhatsApp, has 55 employees serving 450 million customers, and a CEO who's worth $6.8 billion, which would pay about 225,000 store workers $15 an hour for a year.[19]

Manufacturing employment, once the backbone of the middle-class workforce, continued to decline in 2015.[20] The Bureau of Labor Statistics determined that 18 percent of all displaced workers in 2011–13 had been in manufacturing. Just 25 years ago, GM, Ford, and Chrysler generated a combined $36 billion in revenue while employing over a million workers. Today Apple, Facebook, and Google generate over a trillion dollars in revenue with 137,000 workers.[21]

Companies in retail make healthy profits of up to several thousands of dollars per employee. But that pales in comparison to corporations in technology and pharmaceuticals: Apple makes over $500,000 per employee; Facebook and Google are both over $300,000; Merck and Allergan and Pfizer are all well over $100,000.[22] Especially in technology, fewer and fewer employees are needed, as outsourcing continues and as new technological advancements take the place of manufacturing and customer service personnel.

## AI

Robots are *invading the workplace* in a way that wouldn't have seemed possible a few years ago. Restaurants are being designed with no waitstaff or busboys.[23] Amazon is training robots to choose and deliver items from the warehouse shelves.[24] Fedex is preparing for fleets of delivery drones manned by a few operators at workstations. Car manufacturing is being done by 3-D printing. Full-size bridges are being 3-D printed. An entire building was erected in Dubai with a 3-D printer.[25] Vegetable farms can use robots to plant seeds, water the plants, harvest the produce, and even alert humans if a plant isn't growing properly.[26] In Japan, the Henn-na Hotel (meaning "strange hotel") is staffed almost entirely by automated desk clerks, bellhops, and porters.[27]

Technology has begun to diminish the need for bank tellers, cashiers, travel agents, chefs, traffic cops, bartenders, bellhops, maids, pizza delivery people, and even lifeguards. Most stock trading is done by computer. The *driverless vehicle* is coming soon, perhaps sooner than expected,[28] and that means not only a reduction in professional drivers,[29] but also a downsizing of the auto insurance industry. Some high-level professionals are also at risk of being replaced:[30] surgeons, architects, hiring personnel, lawyers, financial and sports journalists, and even the clergy.[31] Robot "teachers" are interacting with students in Japan and the UK.[32] An extensive Citi/Oxford report estimates that nearly half of all jobs in the U.S. are susceptible to automation, 77 percent in China.[33]

Robots are even being designed to help patients stand up and walk away from their hospital beds.[34] The National Science Foundation has begun to develop the *Adaptive Robotic Nurse Assistant*.[35]

Researchers at the University of Chicago have estimated that half of the labor decline in this century is due to the replacement of people by computers and software.[36]

Machines have risen, to take it a step further, from blue-collar to white-collar status. They are artificially *intelligent*. And, as *The Economist* reminds us: "Robots don't complain, or demand higher wages, or kill themselves."[37]

## Sharing in the Downsizing

Free-market enthusiasts look to the sharing economy (or "gig" economy, or "day labor" economy) for salvation, with companies like Uber and Airbnb and TaskRabbit enabling the dreams of Millennials, who, according to *Time*'s Rana Foroohar, "want to be their own boss...any Uber driver will tell you that having totally flexible hours is the best part of the gig." But at the same time, Uber workers have no employee benefits. Thus, says Foroohar, "the company also captures all the fear of the broken social compact in America."[38]

The sharing economy is itself a product of a new technology, social networking, which is sustained by the cooperative efforts of many people, and which provides a platform for the dissemination of information and responsiveness vital to new youth-oriented industries. Uber takes full advantage.[39] The company, with a market valuation of $50 billion, has 4,000 employees, along with 160,000 drivers who are not considered by the company to be employees. This is not a horizontal sharing process, but rather a hierarchical control structure, with tens of thousands of American workers denied the traditional employee support system.

In the case of Airbnb, capitalism extends its sticky tentacles into the pleasant-sounding "home-sharing" mix, as commercial real-estate operators have moved in, evading long-established local housing laws to squeeze out lower-income tenants in favor of high-paying night-by-night customers.[40]

The sharing economy has created companies that promote their employees' independence while denying them health and retirement benefits, sick pay, overtime pay, and vacation pay.[41] It's not a new capitalist idea. Merck and *Out Magazine* are among the companies that have "outsourced" employee positions to independent contractor positions in the past, either by a mass layoff or by selling part of the company, after which former employees could be hired back at lower pay and without benefits.

The sharing economy is actually just a small part—at least so far—of the "alternative work" environment that is dominated by independent and employer-hired contract workers in manufacturing, health care, education, legal work, and public administration. These aren't Uber-like "on demand" jobs, but they're equally lacking in the security of traditional employer–employee relationships. And such positions are growing fast.[42]

The concept of being one's own boss has an appealing ring to it, until it is recognized that the great majority of workers are more comfortable and productive in a traditional employer–employee relationship based on steady wages for scheduled labor. Sharing our time and space and working arrangements with each other is not generally an option. Not many of us are prepared to offer Uber rides or TaskRabbit services, or to rent out our living spaces to strangers. We welcome privacy, we demand regular patterns in our day-to-day work activities, and we need the security of a steady income in return for our efforts.

Politico writers[43] assure us that "There's an easily available job for just about everyone in the gig economy." That may be so, at low wages. But a workable transition from an employment-based to a gig-based economy, with living wages and reasonable benefits, will take years of planning for our slow-moving, conflict-ridden society. And a capitalist system has little incentive to help provide "gigs" for the people most in need of employment.

## Sharing in a Cooperative Way

Yet sharing may work after all, if a "co-op" element is built into it. "Crowd-based capitalism"[44] may actually help empower workers rather than disenfranchise them, even in the ride-sharing business, where, for example, an Uber challenger called **Swift** is owned and managed by the drivers themselves,[45] and a worker-owned and unionized co-op called **Green Taxi** is being formed by over 600 drivers.[46]

Cooperatives represent a form of social democracy that is 100 percent American.[47] Gar Alperovitz describes the process of "decentralizing power, changing the flow of power to localities rather than to the center."[48] The Evergreen Cooperative[49] in Cleveland, the public Bank of North Dakota, the Tennessee Valley Authority, and the Chattanooga internet service are all examples of the **distributed popular control** of essential services.[50] The approach works. At the national level, it will work for the guaranteed income.

## Notes

1 Thompson, Derek, "A World Without Work." *The Atlantic*, July–August, 2015.
2 "An Unbalanced Recovery." National Employment Law Project, August 18, 2014.
3 Stilwell, Victoria, "Manufacturing in U.S. Contracts at Fastest Pace Since 2009." Bloomberg Business, December 1, 2015.
4 Harris, Dan, "China's Golden Age for Foreign Companies is Over." China Law Blog, March 15, 2015.
5 Rosenmann, Alexandra, "Robot Takeover? Get Creative, Chomsky Says." Alternet, June 26, 2016.
6 Autor, David H. and Dorn, David and Hanson, Gordon H., "The China Shock: Learning from Labor Market Adjustment to Large Changes in Trade." National Bureau of Economic Research, January 2016.
7 Gordon, Robert J., *The Rise and Fall of American Growth: The U.S. Standard of Living since the Civil War*. Princeton University Press, 2016.
8 McArdle, Megan, "Don't Blame Americans for Blaming China." Bloomberg View, January 27, 2016.
9 Uchitelle, Louis, *The Disposable American: Layoffs and Their Consequences*. Vintage, 2007.
10 Derber, Charles and Magrass, Yale R., *The Surplus American: How the 1% is Making Us Redundant*. Paradigm, 2012.
11 Zumbrun, Josh, "Post-Recession Job Growth Coming in High-Wage Positions." *Wall Street Journal*, August 17, 2015.
12 Katz, Lawrence F. and Krueger, Alan B., "The Rise and Nature of Alternative Work Arrangements in the United States, 1995–2015." Harvard University, Princeton University, and NBER, March 29, 2016.
13 DePillis, Lydia, "What we Know about the People Who Clean the Floors in Silicon Valley." *Washington Post*, March 30, 2016.
14 "Income and Wage Gaps across the US." U.S. Conference of Mayors, August 2014.
15 "The Low-Wage Recovery." National Employment Law Project, April 2014.
16 Kiersz, Andy, "Low Wage Job Growth is Accelerating." *Business Insider*, March 16, 2015; Gongloff, Mark, "Half of All Jobs Created in The Past 3 Years Were Low-Paying: Study." *Huffington Post*, May 13, 2013; King, Neil, Jr., "Amid Upbeat Economic News, Many Reasons for Pause." *Wall Street Journal*, June 12, 2014.

17 Frohlich, Thomas C., "America's 10 Highest-Paying Companies." MSN Money, April 7, 2015.

18 Thompson, Derek, "A World Without Work." Op. cit.

19 Olson, Parmy, "Exclusive: The Rags-to-Riches Tale of How Jan Koum Built WhatsApp into Facebook's New $19 Billion Baby." Forbes/Tech, February 19, 2014.

20 Stilwell, Victoria, "Manufacturing." Op. cit.

21 Thompson, Cadie, "We've Reached a Tipping Point where Technology is Now Destroying More Jobs than it Creates, Researcher Warns." *Business Insider*, June 3, 2015.

22 "Net Income per Employee." CSIMarket.com, accessed May 31, 2016.

23 Steinmetz, Katy, "Why Your Fast Food is about to Come Even Faster." *Time*, September 24, 2015.

24 Eidelson, Josh and Soper, Spencer, "How Amazon Shames Warehouse Workers to Discourage Theft." MSN Money, March 7, 2016.

25 Whittaker, G. Clay, "Dubai Has 3D-Printed an Entire Building." *Popular Science*, May 26, 2016.

26 Garfield, Leanna, "The World's First Robot-Run Farm Will Harvest 30,000 Heads of Lettuce Daily." *Tech Insider*, January 27, 2016.

27 "A Hotel Run by Robots." *The Week*, June 10, 2016.

28 Chafkin, Max, "Uber's First Self-Driving Fleet Arrives in Pittsburgh this Month." Bloomberg Businessweek, August 18, 2016.

29 Solon, Olivia, "Self-Driving Trucks: What's the Future for America's 3.5 Million Truckers?" *The Guardian*, June 17, 2016.

30 Sherman, Erik, "5 White-Collar Jobs Robots Already Have Taken." *Fortune*, February 25, 2015; Egan, Matt, "Robots Threaten These 8 Jobs." *CNN Money*, May 14, 2015.

31 Susskind, Richard and Susskind, Daniel, *The Future of the Professions: How Technology Will Transform the Work of Human Experts.* Oxford University Press, 2016; Turner, Karen, "Meet 'Ross,' the Newly Hired Legal Robot." *Washington Post*, May 16, 2016.

32 "21 Jobs Where Robots are Already Replacing Humans." *Love Money*, July 20, 2016.

33 "Technology at Work, v2.0." Citi GPS and Oxford University, January 2016.

34 Herships, Sally, "Japan's Long-Term Care Dilemma: Immigrants or Robots?" Marketplace.org, January 25, 2016.

35 Harrington, Elizabeth, "Feds Spend $999,946 Building Robot Nurses." *Washington Free Beacon*, January 13, 2016.

36 Thompson, Derek, "A World Without Work." Op. cit.

37 "Robots Don't Complain. Or Demand Higher Wages, or Kill Themselves." *The Economist*, August 6, 2011.

38 Foroohar, Rana, "In the New World of Work, Is Uber the Villain or a Hero?" *Time*, December 9, 2015.

39 Hargreaves, Steve, "Uber Driver Is, in Fact, an Employee." *CNN Money*, June 17, 2015; Owens, Jeremy C., "Three Numbers Travis Kalanick Revealed about Uber." *Market Watch*, September 16, 2015.

40 Hill, Steven, "Airbnb's Tricky New Numbers Game." Salon.com, December 3, 2015.

41 Chen, Michelle, "This Is How Bad the Sharing Economy Is for Workers." *The Nation*, September 14, 2015.

42  Katz, Lawrence F. and Krueger, Alan B., Op. cit.; Sussman, Anna Louie and Zumbrun, Josh, "Contract Workforce Outpaces Growth in Silicon-Valley Style 'Gig' Jobs." *Wall Street Journal*, March 25, 2016.

43  Conda, Cesar and Khanna, Derek, "Uber for Welfare." *Politico*, January 27, 2016.

44  Sundararajan, Arun, *The Sharing Economy: The End of Employment and the Rise of Crowd-Based Capitalism.* MIT Press, 2016.

45  Foroohar, Rana, "How the Gig Economy Could Save Capitalism." *Time*, June 15, 2016.

46  Hansen, Mary, "What If Uber Were a Unionized, Worker-Owned Co-Op? These Denver Cabbies Are Making It Happen." *Yes! Magazine*, April 10, 2015.

47  Kaye, Harvey J., "Social Democracy Is 100% American." Bill Moyers & Co., July 3, 2015.

48  Alperovitz, Gar, *What Then Must We Do? Straight Talk about the Next American Revolution.* Chelsea Green, 2013.

49  Alperovitz, Gar; Williamson, Thad; and Howard, Ted, "The Cleveland Model." *The Nation*, February 11, 2010.

50  Alperovitz, Gar and Hanna, Thomas, "Socialism, American-Style." *New York Times*, July 23, 2015.

## Bibliography

Barnes, Peter, *With Liberty and Dividends for All: How to Save Our Middle Class When Jobs Don't Pay Enough.* Berrett-Koehler, 2014.

Bregman, Rutger and Manton, Elizabeth, *Utopia for Realists: The Case for a Universal Basic Income, Open Borders, and a 15-Hour Workweek.* The Correspondent, 2016.

Bryjolfsson, Erik and McAfee, Andrew, *The Second Machine Age: Work, Progress, and Prosperity in a Time of Brilliant Technologies.* W.W. Norton & Company, 2014.

Ford, Martin, *Rise of the Robots: Technology and the Threat of a Jobless Future.* Basic Books, 2015.

Raventos, Daniel, *Basic Income: The Material Conditions of Freedom.* Pluto Press, 2007.

Rifkin, Jeremy, *The End of Work.* Putnam Publishing Group, 1995.

Stern, Andy, *Raising the Floor: How a Universal Basic Income Can Renew Our Economy and Rebuild the American Dream.* PublicAffairs, 2016.

Sundararajan, Arun, *The Sharing Economy: The End of Employment and the Rise of Crowd-Based Capitalism.* MIT Press, 2016.

# 3

# CHILDREN

## The Past: Pennsylvania *Breaker Boys*[1]

The breaker boys were 8- to 14-year-olds who were forced to leave the playgrounds and the fresh air to work ten hours a day, six days a week, breaking slabs of coal into smaller pieces. They sat in wooden seats in front of bins fed by conveyor belts, in a dark cavern of a mine filled with a constant haze of coal dust.

The hazards of their job are beyond belief. The boys were forbidden to wear gloves because of the need to feel for impurities in the coal, and as a result they went home with fingernails ground to nubs and their hands black with soot and dust and blood. Some lost fingers, or even arms and legs, in the gears of the conveyor belts. At times, a boy would get dragged into the coal piles where he was smothered or crushed to death. Their bodies might not be found until the machines were stopped at the end of the day.

Even if they survived with limbs intact, the breaker boys were likely to get black lung disease from the constant breathing of thick coal dust. It was a hellish existence for young boys. They couldn't slow down, because an overlord stood behind them with a whip, and they couldn't quit because most were helping to support their families.

In addition to breakers there were "spraggers," who ran alongside rail cars in the barely illuminated mine shafts, jabbing pole-like sprags into the wheels to control their speed. If not done correctly, cars could jump the track and crush the spragger against the mine walls.

There were also "nippers," who sat alone in an isolated section of the mine for ten hours, with only oil headlamps to break the darkness as they waited to open a ventilator door for incoming rail cars pulled by mules. One can only imagine the feelings of desolation that took over their young minds.

**FIGURE 3.1** Breaker boys. Hughestown Borough Coal Co., Pittston, PA, January 16, 1911.

National Archives, Lewis W. Hine collection (http://arlweb.msha.gov/CENTURY/LITTLE/PAGE4.asp).

**FIGURE 3.2** Breaker boys. Hughestown Borough Coal Co., Pittston, PA, January 16, 1911.

National Archives, Lewis W. Hine collection (http://arlweb.msha.gov/CENTURY/LITTLE/PAGE2.asp).

Child labor went well beyond the mines. Children had worked on farms since colonial times. But with the Industrial Revolution they became a great business asset in many other ways, cheaper and easier to control, and less likely to go on strike. They were small enough to get through chimneys, poorly enough paid to shine shoes or peddle cheap goods such as matches or flowers, wretched enough to work as the "sweepers" who removed horse manure from the streets. They worked at the fiery furnaces of glass factories, the metal-stamping machines of canneries, the fast-spinning looms of textile firms. Saddest of all, some were put to work as prostitutes.

Children usually had no alternative, since their families depended on the income, especially if parents were placed in debtors' prison. When parents couldn't support their children, they occasionally turned them over to a factory owner. The children were only paid 10–20 percent of an adult's wage. It wasn't unusual for a child to work 16 hours a day. And escape was generally not an option: a glass factory in Massachusetts was surrounded by barbed wire "to keep the young imps inside."

The mid nineteenth century saw attempts at reform, but a massive influx of immigrants from Ireland and other countries, along with the ever-expanding growth of industry, kept the children in the factories. Then along came "Mother Jones."[2] Called "the most dangerous woman in America" by a U.S. district attorney, Mary Harris Jones battled industrialists on behalf of workers and children, welcoming all comers to march behind her, including blacks and mothers armed with mops and brooms. She exclaimed, "Every day little children came into Union Headquarters, some with their hands off, some with the thumb missing, some with their fingers off at the knuckle. They were stooped little things, round shouldered and skinny." She marched with children whose picket signs said, "We want to go to school! 55 hours or nothing!" Yes, children were striking for a 55-hour week.

Mother Jones took striking children all the way to President Teddy Roosevelt's Long Island home in 1903, telling the newspapers who refused to publicize her protest, "Well, I've got stock in these little children and I'll arrange a little publicity." The president refused to meet with her, but her demands finally brought the issue to the public's attention.

**FIGURE 3.3** Breaker boys sort coal in South Pittston, Pennsylvania, in 1911.
National Archives, Lewis W. Hine collection (https://commons.wikimedia.org/wiki/File:Pennsylvania_breaker_boys_1911.jpg).

## The Present: Disposable Children[3]

It may be the greatest hypocrisy of America's conservative leaders, that they demand control over a woman's body, but then show disturbing patterns of neglect after a child comes into the world. It can go beyond neglect to disdain for the poor. In a perversely unequal nation in which the well-off blame destitute people for their own struggles, the children of the poor become the innocent victims.

Children of all ages are deemed disposable.

### *For Every $10 Million Family, a Homeless Child*

And it's getting worse. For every TWO homeless children in 2007, there are now THREE.[4] There are sixteen million children living on $5 a day for food.[5] Half of America's public school kids qualify for subsidized lunches.[6]

Yet spending on children's programs recently declined for the first time in nearly 20 years.[7]

There's something fundamentally wrong with a society that allows a hedge fund manager to make a **billion dollars** while House Republicans attempt to cut back on lunches for over three million children.[8]

Financier and CEO Peter Schiff said, "People don't go hungry in a capitalist economy." But the sixteen million children on food stamps know what it's like to go hungry. Perhaps, some in Congress would say those children should be working. "There is no such thing as a free lunch," insisted Georgia Representative Jack Kingston, even for schoolchildren, who should be required to "sweep the floor of the cafeteria" (as they actually do at a charter school in Oregon).[9]

The problems don't end for children when they're given a home. Teacher Sonya Romero-Smith told about the two little homeless girls she adopted: "Getting rid of bedbugs, that took us a while. Night terrors, that took a little while. Hoarding food."[10]

In America, black parents are often blamed for family dysfunction, especially "absent fathers." But research refutes the myth, as the Pew Research Center[11] found little difference between white and black fathers, and the Centers for Disease Control[12] found that black fathers are in many ways more involved with their kids than fathers in other racial groups.

### *School Kids Living in "Combat Zones"*

That's a description from Henry Giroux, who refers to schools as "combat zones where it is routine for many students to be subjected to metal detectors, surveillance cameras, uniformed security guards, weapons searches, and in some cases SWAT team raids and police dogs sniffing for drugs."[13]

Students are "no longer viewed as a social investment in the future." Instead, with almost two-thirds of middle schools and high schools employing "school resource officers," the students—disproportionately minority children—are being redirected to the criminal justice system.[14] The criminalizing reaches absurd levels:[15]

- Students *throwing peanuts* on a school bus being arrested for felony assault after a peanut hit the bus driver.
- A police officer repeatedly *hitting a student* with a police baton, claiming it was "reasonable and necessary," receiving no punishment.
- A student suspended for being a "danger to the staff." He was *three years old*.

With the attack on public schools, education "reformers," who have a lot of money but little knowledge of the real world of education, have moved in to privatize, in effect turning each child into a marketable product. They "starve the beast" in order to turn education into a business. They frighten America with words from people like Rupert Murdoch: "The failure rates of our public schools represent a tragic waste of human capital that is making America less competitive."[16] They've convinced many Americans that charter schools provide "freedom" of choice and a better-quality education.

Big business models are inappropriate for the education of children.[17] As the following discussion will show, the development of social skills at an early age is the key to success later in life, and that requires nurturing rather than profit-making.

## "Fixing" Our Educational System

### K-12 Education is Getting Worse

A shocking new OECD report says that among developed countries the U.S. has the highest percentage of youths aged 16–19 with low numeric skills, and the third-highest percentage with low literacy skills.[18]

SAT scores in 2015 were the lowest since the test was revised in 2005. Math scores for fourth-graders and eighth-graders dropped for the first time since the tests were first administered in 1990.[19]

### Market "Reform" Isn't Working[20]

The unsatisfactory results, according to the *Washington Post*, "reflect a troubling shortcoming of education-reform efforts."[21]

Technology-based instruction is apparently doing more harm than good. An analysis of "Programme for International Student Assessment" (PISA) scores led to the conclusion that "While PISA results suggest that limited use of computers at school may be better than not using computers at all, using them more intensively than the current OECD average tends to be associated with significantly poorer student performance."[22] The American Statistical Association cautioned against the use of standardized student test scores for teacher evaluations.[23] Online instruction, not surprisingly, is likely the worst form of schooling, as suggested by Stanford's CREDO researchers: "Innovative new research suggests that students of online charter schools had significantly weaker academic performance in math and reading, compared with their counterparts in conventional schools."[24]

Education must go from STEM to STEAM, with the Arts included along with science, technology, engineering, and math. A study at Michigan State University found that "success in science is accompanied by developed ability in other fields such as the fine arts."[25] According to a 2007 report in the *Journal for Research in Music Education*, students in high-quality music programs scored 19 percent higher in English and 17 percent higher in mathematics than those without a music program.[26] Both the College Entrance Examination Board and the National Association of Music Education found that music programs improved SAT scores later on.[27]

## The Three Big Sins of Charter Schools

Charter schools generally perform no better than public schools, as summarized by the nonpartisan Spencer Foundation and Public Agenda: "There is very little evidence that charter and traditional public schools differ meaningfully in their average impact on students' standardized test performance."[28] Yet, in at least three ways, charters undermine and debase the educational system that they profess to serve:

1. **Committing Fraud:** In 2015, they wasted an estimated $1.4 billion of taxpayer money through "financial fraud, waste, abuse, and mismanagement."
2. **Lacking Transparency:** The Center for Media and Democracy calls them a "black hole" into which the federal government has dumped an outrageous $3.7 billion over two decades, with little accountability to the public.[29]
3. **Discarding Students:** Prominent New York charter network Success Academy has frequently been accused of "counseling out" students who are low-performing, disruptive, or otherwise difficult to teach.[30] Even worse are charters that shut down, stranding hundreds of students, while their business operators can just move on to their next project. Nearly 2,500 charter schools closed their doors from 2001 to 2013, leaving over a quarter of a million kids temporarily without a school.

## Public Education Works if It's Supported

The National Bureau of Economic Research found that a ten percent increase in per-pupil spending leads to higher earnings and less poverty for children from poor families.[31] The Shanker Institute concurs, concluding from several studies that "On average, aggregate measures of per-pupil spending are positively associated with improved or higher student outcomes."[32]

Yet public education is NOT being supported. The Center on Budget and Policy Priorities (CBPP) recently stated: "Most states provide less support per student for elementary and secondary schools—in some cases, much less—than before the Great Recession...Worse, some states are still cutting eight years after the recession took hold."[33]

Many of our nation's biggest corporations aren't paying the state taxes that should be funding our public schools.[34] Evidence comes from Good Jobs First[35] and the *New York Times*,[36] reporting on 2011–12 data:

* Federal, state, and local governments give up *$170 billion per year* in tax incentives to the corporate world.
* States were forced to cut education and other public services and raise taxes by a collective *$156 billion* in 2011.
* The subsidy cost per job averaged *$456,000* for 170 "megadeals" analyzed in 2013 by Good Jobs First.

Most damaging for public education may be the cutbacks to preschool programs, which have been shown by numerous studies to provide the *social and emotional* foundations for lifelong skills, and for higher earnings, especially for disadvantaged children.[37] Yet in 2013, Head Start was hit with the worst cutbacks in its history.

Over half of America's four-year-olds are NOT attending preschool.[38] We're near the bottom of the developed world in the percentage of four-year-olds in early childhood education.[39]

## Democratic Socialism Works for Education[40]

No, we're not Finland. But we can learn from them. The schools in that country were once considered mediocre at best, but they've achieved a remarkable turnaround by focusing on teachers rather than on testing and technology. Government funding is applied equally to all schools, and classes in the arts are available to all students, and as a result, Finnish students finish at or near the top of international comparisons for literacy and math.

The 1966 Coleman Report,[41] widely considered the most important education study of the twentieth century, concluded that "academic achievement was less related to the quality of a student's school, and more related to the social composition of the school, the student's sense of control of his environment and future, the verbal skills of teachers, and the student's family background."

The key word is "social." Not only at the preschool level, but throughout the years of child development. Even free-market economist Milton Friedman once stepped out of character and agreed: "We have always been proud, and with good reason, of the widespread availability of schooling to all and the role that public schooling has played in…enabling people from different cultural and religious backgrounds to live together in harmony."

Children aren't products to be bought and sold. The profit motive should end at the front door of the public school.

Comparing past to present reminds us that while the oppressive conditions suffered by vulnerable Americans may have changed in method and in ostensible acceptance by the public, they exist today in a more insidious form, one that appears to place the responsibility for their own misfortunes on the parents of children in poverty.

Yes, there's something terribly wrong with a society that allows a billion-dollar hedge fund manager to receive preferential tax treatment while a school lunch program for three million children in poverty is deemed an entitlement that needs to be eliminated.[42]

## Children, Personally[43]

> What the bells of ice cream trucks are to kids in Wilmette, gunshots are to me.
>
> Latoya Winters, 27, Chicago

Latoya Winters is still referred to as "our baby" by some of the elderly local women who knew her as a child. She grew up in East Garfield Park on the west side of Chicago and heard the gangs—which included some of her brothers and cousins and friends—shooting at each other outside her window.

She was raised by her grandmother, Carrie Winters, who also cared for her granddaughter's eight siblings and 10 to 15 cousins, as well as occasional visiting friends who needed a place to stay. Latoya's mother was a drug addict. Grandma had a two-flat building, with plenty of room for the kids to sprawl on the beds or curl up with blankets on the floor.

The once-peaceful neighborhood at Jackson and California became a center for gangs when the wealthy families moved out and took local businesses and jobs with them. The Gangster Disciples ruled, pressuring young boys to adopt their way of life—and death. Latoya "talked to people like my uncles and cousins and brothers who say, 'I got put into the gang when I was younger,' and, 'If I could have gotten out, I would have.'"

The litany of tragedies in Latoya's young life is difficult to comprehend. In the early morning hours of May 7, 1997, as the eight-year-old entered her sisters' room to look for her shoes, flames burst out of the walls, perhaps fueled by the sudden draft of air through the doorway. Thick black smoke poured into the air around her. In an instant, she was screaming for everyone to wake up, and then joining the chaotic rush of family members running for safety. Two of her sisters never got out. Firefighters found six-year-old Bernadine and ten-year-old Amiya still hugging each other under the bed.

Then came the shootings. In 1997, the same year as the fire, two 16-year-olds, one a next-door neighbor, were killed in a drive-by shooting. Latoya was awakened one night two years later by heavy pounding on the front door. Her 16-year-old cousin Lorenzo fell into the room, covered with blood from gunshot wounds. He survived. But three months later, his mother Linda was shot and killed just a few short blocks west of the Winters' west-side home.

On a spring evening in 2001, when Latoya was 12, she was startled by a sudden clamor of frantic calls and rushing footsteps outside her bedroom door, and when she hurried outside, family members were gathered together, kneeling over her older brother Lamont. He had been shot repeatedly at close range by rival gang members. Apparently, he had killed someone a week earlier, and now, a day after removing a bulletproof vest from under his jacket, gang retaliation had taken his life.

But two years later, Latoya's cousin Phillip was killed, and a year after that another cousin, Andre, was shot down in front of the two-flat. Today Latoya looks out at the cluttered, weed-filled vacant lot next to her home and struggles to hold back tears: in each case, the killers had ambushed their young victims after hiding in the overgrown lot.

In 2002, Latoya's sister was killed in a motorcycle accident. "So it was every year," she reflects, "we lost someone."

The neighborhood's safe havens were Calhoun Public School, a "generational" institution just a block from Jackson and California, and Marillac House on the next block, run by the Daughters of Charity, staffed by scores of local residents and volunteers, and offering after-school programs, adult classes, and pre-K. Latoya found a new way of life at Marillac. "I became involved in everything you can name, just to have something positive to do. I played basketball, I played volleyball, I did poetry, I did choir—you name it, I did it. As soon as I walked into Marillac, it felt like home." Indeed, Marillac reflects the strength of community, the pride and dignity of people whose efforts are too often overshadowed by the destructive actions of a few deprived and desperate young people.

With a recommendation from the Marillac directors, Latoya was given the opportunity to attend Regina Dominican High School in north suburban Wilmette. She lived in a group home, benefited from grief counseling, perfected her writing and speaking skills, and was so admired by classmates that she was elected Student Council President in her senior year.

But the worst memories of childhood flooded back in Latoya's first year of college at Northern Illinois University when a former student killed five people in a shooting rampage. Her up-and-down life took another downward turn in the next school year—her infant son, born with a rare brain disorder, died before his first birthday.

Latoya is now back in East Garfield Park, working at Marillac, pursuing a master's degree in social work at DePaul University, and planning to work with neighborhood youth. The violence around her home is less frequent now, partly because nearby gentrification has brought with it a greater degree of police watchfulness. But violence still happens. In July, 2014 a bullet came through the bedroom window where 11-year-old Shamiya Adams was playing with friends at a sleepover. She was hit in the head and died the next morning.

Latoya believes she has known almost a hundred people killed by guns in her 27 years. But she is like the many volunteers and employees at Marillac, always optimistic and always feeling "blessed" for what they have. After all, as one of them pointed out, "We're just like anyone else, except we don't have money and we don't have jobs."

Twenty years before Latoya was born, on the west side of Chicago in 1968, during the riots after the assassination of Martin Luther King, a group of nuns stood on the roof of a building, watching the city burn around them. In the end, their one square block of the inner city remained untouched, as if surrounded by an invisible shield impenetrable to fire and gunshots and looters. This was Marillac House. For over a hundred years, the Daughters of Charity have served as guardians and partners and mentors and comforters to the community, providing childcare, counseling young mothers, supplementing nutritional needs, and securing seniors and the disabled. Today, as in 1968, even as gentrification gradually transforms segments of Chicago's west side, most of the area remains impoverished, and Marillac continues to be the soul of the community.

Memories came flooding back to Deanna, one of the staff members at Marillac. At a Saturday afternoon 2014 Christmas party for 85 kids at Calhoun School across the street, a boy was shot. Visitors and volunteers were visibly shaken, uncertain what to do, some of them panicking. The neighborhood kids were the most calm. They were veterans of street warfare.

That moment reminded Deanna of another incident at Rockwell Gardens, during a back-to-school summer fair, at an inflatable jumping castle, when shots rang out, hitting the plastic of the bouncy structure, deflating it. The schoolkids took the lead, telling the adult volunteers, "You gotta leave. Now." Adults and kids scrambled to safety through a hole in a fence at the edge of the grounds.

To kids in wealth-secured neighborhoods, a bouncing castle is nothing but fun, with never a thought to violence coming from the outside.

Most important for the kids, of course, was their neighborhood school. Latoya grew up with her friend Jalesa, the two of them attending Calhoun Public School during the day and stepping across the street to Marillac Social Center for after-school activities. Everyone knew each other on those two blocks; kids walked together, to and from school, and in the evenings. Parents—most of whom had gone to Calhoun—knew each other, often through volunteer work at the social center.

In 2013, Calhoun was one of 50 schools closed by Mayor Rahm Emanuel. It was shut down despite a committee recommendation that it remain open. No counseling was provided. CPS board members, few of whom live in the neighborhood, offered no explanations. Jalesa and Latoya, who still work at Marillac as they pursue other career interests, said the children are scattered now. They all take buses to a variety of public and charter schools outside the once-intimate neighborhood. Some have to walk a few blocks; some have to cross busy streets. None of them gather together before and after school, as they used to do on the grounds of Calhoun.

One of Marillac's directors recalled, "I went to all those meetings where the recommendation was NOT to close Calhoun...the Board listed 13 schools that shouldn't be closed, and Calhoun was one of them. When we went in front of the council, it was one vote and one is done...Charter schools now...make money on the backs of children."

## Notes

1  Miller, Donald, "The Breaker Boys." *America 1900, The American Experience*, Public Broadcasting System.
2  Collins, Gail, "America's Women." The Illinois Labor History Society, 2003.
3  Buchheit, Paul, "Disposable Children." CommonDreams.org, November 9, 2015; Buchheit, Paul, "Five Great American Hypocrisies." NationofChange.org, December 10, 2015; Buchheit, Paul, "The Numbers are Staggering: U.S. is 'World Leader' in Child Poverty." Alternet.org, April 13, 2015; Buchheit, Paul, "A Nation's Shame: Trillions in New Wealth, Millions of Children in Poverty." Truthout/Buzzflash, April 13, 2015.
4  "America's Youngest Outcasts: A Report Card on Child Homelessness." American Institutes for Research, November 2014.
5  "One in Five Children Receive Food Stamps." Census Bureau, February 20, 2015.
6  "A New Majority Research Bulletin: Low Income Students Now a Majority in the Nation's Public Schools." Southern Education Foundation, 2015.
7  "Survey Finds Decline in Child Welfare Spending." *Child Trends*, September 26, 2014.
8  "Top 10 Hedge Fund Chiefs Took Home a Combined $10.07 Billion." *New York Times*, May 10, 2016; Herro, Cory, "House Republicans Want to Cut Free School Lunch Programs." *Think Progress*, April 28, 2016.
9  Piro, Lauren, "Forget Janitors! In This School, the Students Clean Up." *Good Housekeeping*, April 6, 2015.
10  Layton, Lyndsey, "Majority of U.S. Public School Students are in Poverty." *Washington Post*, January 16, 2015.
11  "The New American Father." Pew Research Center, June 14, 2013.
12  Jones, Jo and Mosher, William D., "Fathers' Involvement with Their Children: United States, 2006–2010." *National Health Statistics Reports*, December 20, 2013.
13  Giroux, Henry, "Terrorizing School Children in the American Police State." *Counterpunch*, November 2, 2015.
14  Botelho, Greg and Ellis, Ralph, "Police in Schools: Why are they there?" *CNN*, October 30, 2015.

15  Buchheit, Paul, "Disposable Children." CommonDreams.org, November 09, 2015
16  Rabil, Sarah, "Murdoch Says Education 'Failure Factories' Imperil Middle Class." *Bloomberg*, October 6, 2010.
17  Saltman, Kenneth J. and Gabbard, David, *Education as Enforcement: The Militarization and Corporatization of Schools* (2nd Edition). Routledge, 2010.
18  OECD Skills Studies. *Building Skills for All*, 2016.
19  Strauss, Valerie, "What the National Drop in 2015 NAEP Test Scores Really Means." *Washington Post*, October 28, 2015.
20  Buchheit, Paul, "Five Facts for the Dangerously Deluded Education Reformers." CommonDreams.org, June 30, 2014.
21  Anderson, Nick, "SAT Scores at Lowest Level in 10 Years, Fueling Worries about High Schools." *Washington Post*, September 3, 2015.
22  OECD iLibrary. "Students, Computers and Learning." September 15, 2015.
23  "ASA Statement on Using Value-Added Models for Educational Assessment." American Statistical Association, April 8, 2014.
24  "Online Charter School Students Falling Behind Their Peers." *CREDO*, Stanford University, October 27, 2015.
25  Root-Bernstein, Robert, "Arts Foster Scientific Success." *Journal of Psychology of Science and Technology*, Vol. 1, No. 2, 2008.
26  Johnson, Christopher M. and Memmott, Jenny E., "Examination of Relationship between Participation in School Music Programs of Differing Quality and Standardized Test Results." *MENC Journal of Research in Music Education*, Winter 2006, Vol. 54, No. 4, pp. 293–307.
27  "Benefits of Music." National Education Music Company.
28  "Charter Schools in Perspective." A Joint Project of the Spencer Foundation and Public Agenda, 2015.
29  "Charter School Black Hole." The Center for Media and Democracy, October 2015.
30  Taylor, Kate, "At a Success Academy Charter School, Singling Out Pupils Who Have 'Got to Go.'" *New York Times*, October 30, 2015.
31  Jackson, C. Kirabo; Johnson, Rucker C.; Persico, Claudia: "The Effects of School Spending on Educational and Economic Outcomes: Evidence from School Finance Reforms." National Bureau of Economic Research, January 2015.
32  Baker, Bruce D., "Does Money Matter in Education?" Albert Shanker Institute, 2016.
33  Leachman, Michael; Albares, Nick; Masterson, Kathleen; Wallace, Marlana, "Most States Have Cut School Funding, and Some Continue Cutting." Center on Budget and Policy Priorities, January 25, 2016.
34  Personal research from SEC data (www.youdeservefacts.org/20160404.xls), accessed April 4, 2016.
35  Mattera, Philip; Tarczynska, Kasia; LeRoy, Greg, "Megadeals: The Largest Economic Development Subsidy Packages Ever Awarded by State and Local Governments in the United States." *Good Jobs First*, June 2013 (updated December 2015).
36  Story, Louise, "As Companies Seek Tax Deals, Governments Pay High Price." *New York Times*, December 1, 2012.
37  "NIEER Statement on President Obama's Pre-K Proposal." National Institute for Early Education Research, February 14, 2013.

38 "State Trends in Child Well-Being." Annie E. Casey Foundation, KIDS COUNT Project, 2015.

39 "Education at a Glance: OECD Indicators 2012." Organisation for Economic Co-operation and Development, 2012.

40 Buchheit, Paul, "Why We Need Democratic Socialism to Fix Our Educational System." CommonDreams.org, February 22, 2016.

41 Coleman, James S., *Equality of Educational Opportunity*. National Center for Educational Statistics, 1966.

42 "Top 10 Hedge Fund Chiefs Took Home a Combined $10.07 Billion." *New York Times*, May 10, 2016; Herro, Cory, "House Republicans Want to Cut Free School Lunch Programs." Think Progress, April 28, 2016.

43 "People Issue 2012: Latoya Winters, the Graduate." *Chicago Reader*, December 19, 2012; Bogira, Steve, "In Chicago's War Zones, the Tragedy Extends Beyond the Kids Who Die." *Chicago Reader*, August 20, 2014; Winters, Latoya, "You Live by It, You Die by It." Big Shoulders Books, October 18, 2013.

## Bibliography

Coleman, James S., *Equality of Educational Opportunity*. National Center for Educational Statistics, 1966.

Erickson, Megan, *Class War: The Privatization of Childhood*. Verso, 2015.

Kotlowitz, Alex, *There Are No Children Here: The Story of Two Boys Growing Up in the Other America*. Doubleday, 1992.

Lamy, Cynthia E., *American Children in Chronic Poverty: Complex Risks, Benefit-Cost Analyses, and Untangling the Knot*. Lexington Books, 2012.

Putnam, Robert, *Our Kids: The American Dream in Crisis*. Simon & Schuster, 2015.

Ravitch, Diane, *The Death and Life of the Great American School System: How Testing and Choice Are Undermining Education*. Basic Books, 2011.

Saltman, Kenneth J., *The Failure of Corporate School Reform (Critical Interventions: Politics, Culture and the Promise of Democracy)*. Paradigm Publishers, 2013.

# 4

# THE POOR

## The Past: The Wrath of Poverty[1]

On Easter Sunday, April 21, 1935, the people of southeast Colorado huddled together in their homes, waiting out a violent dust storm. It was typical of the numerous "black blizzards" occurring across the entire stretch of the Great Plains, from Canada to Texas.

Week after week the dust accumulated, forming layers like a sandy desert, with dunes and drifts blocking doorways, forcing some families to enter and exit through their windows. Homeowners tried to block the cracks in window sills and doorways with wet sheets, or with rags and heavy tape. But the dust made it through anyway. It got in the food, it got swallowed, it left tiny flecks of grit lodged in the teeth. People were spitting up clods of dirt the size of a fountain pen. Schoolchildren had trouble breathing through the facemasks that they were required to wear.

"The impact is like a shovelful of fine sand flung against the face," wrote Avis D. Carlson in the *New Republic*. "People caught in their own yards grope for the doorstep. Cars come to a standstill, for no light in the world can penetrate that swirling murk...We live with the dust, eat it, sleep with it."

It had started a decade earlier, when the price of wheat was rising, and farmers flooded the western plains with the hope of quick riches. Soon tractors were everywhere, like giant metal insects, ripping up prairie sod, harvesting twenty times faster than farmers had done with horse and plow. J.R. Davison of Oklahoma remembered: "So everybody got him a John Deere tractor or an old International and really went to plowin' this country and my dad was no different than the rest of 'em. You know, he'd run that thing all day and when the sun went down, why, he'd come in and do the chores and I'd go runnin' that tractor 'til morning."

**FIGURE 4.1** Dust storm near Beaver, Oklahoma in 1935.
National Archives, Franklin D. Roosevelt Library (https://commons.wikimedia.org/wiki/File:Dust_
Storms,_%22Dust_Storm_Near_Beaver,_Oklahoma%22_-_NARA_-_195354.tif).

**FIGURE 4.2** Dust storm approaching Stratford, Texas in 1935.
NOAA George E. Marsh Album, theb1365, Historic C&GS Collection (https://commons.
wikimedia.org/wiki/File:Dust_Storm_Texas_1935.jpg).

No one noticed the steady increase of dusty swirls dancing across the wheat fields. Prairie grass was gone in most places, taking with it the deep roots, and the stability, that had held the land together. In 1931, the rains stopped. Crops withered. The dust got worse every day. It was changing lives. Margie Daniels of Oklahoma said, "I can remember looking at Dad and he'd be laid back in his big chair, his old lounge chair, you know, with his feet up and usually one of the kids on his lap. But he would just be, you know, kinda lookin' off into space." In 1934, with supplies of livestock feed depleted, the federal government bought up starving cattle to put them out of their misery.

When it seemed conditions couldn't get any worse, another plague swept the Oklahoma land, as hundreds of thousands of starving jack rabbits came to devour everything that remained. Residents organized rabbit drives: they'd surround bunches of rabbits, drive them into pens, and then club them to death. Margie Daniels recalled with displeasure: "You could hear the rabbits screaming you know. That's what was scary to me. I think that sound affected everyone. I know it sounded terrible to me as a little girl. And you know I'd think sounds like a baby cryin' or squealin', or, you know, being hurt. It was really sad." But there was no other way to save the dwindling remnants of a garden.

Out of desperation, the Okies and the Arkies headed west, mostly for California, sending more new settlers to that state than the gold rush. John Steinbeck wrote in *The Grapes of Wrath*:

> And then the dispossessed were drawn west…Car-loads, caravans, homeless and hungry…They streamed over the mountains, hungry and restless— restless as ants, scurrying to find work to do—to lift, to push, to pull, to pick, to cut—anything, any burden to bear, for food. The kids are hungry. We got no place to live…

In March of 1936, U.S. photographer Dorothea Lange, on her way to San Francisco after searching the countryside for Depression-era photos, passed a sign saying "Pea-Pickers' Camp" in Nipomo, California. Thinking little of it, she drove on. But a few miles down the road, she changed her mind and turned back. Her first encounter in the camp was with a widowed 32-year-old Oklahoma mother of seven who had driven to California looking for work. Now, after a storm had wiped out the crop, and after she had sold the tires from her car to buy food, she sat under a makeshift tent with her children, unprepared for the days ahead of them. Florence Owens Thompson was only 32, looked like 52.

Days later, a *San Francisco News* article reported: "Ragged, Hungry, Broke, Harvest Workers Live in Squalor." Shocked Californians immediately began sending food, and the family of "migrant mother" Florence Owens Thompson found refuge in a government shelter.

**FIGURE 4.3** Florence Owens Thompson, "Migrant Mother," Pea-Pickers' Camp, Nipomo, California, 1936.
Photography of Dorothea Lange (https://commons.wikimedia.org/wiki/File:Migrant_agricultural_worker%27s_family,_Nipomo,_California_ppmsca03054u.jpg).

## The Present Day: The Living Poor

*Of the half-billion poorest adults in the world, one out of twenty is an American.*

That seems impossible, with so many extremely poor countries, and it requires a second look at the data,[2] and then a third look. But it's true. In the world's poorest decile (bottom 10 percent), one out of twenty are Americans, many of whom are burdened with *so much debt* that any remnant of tangible wealth is negated. Other nations have high debt, most notably in Europe, but without an excessive burden on their poorest citizens.

Incredibly, then, about 22 million of America's 243 million adults are part of the world's poorest 10 percent. In contrast, over 110 million American adults are among the world's richest 10 percent.

## The 8-Step Process to Wipe Out the Poor Half of America[3]

*Happy Monday! S&P 500 now up 10% for year—CNN Money[4]*
*Third-quarter U.S. economic growth strongest in 11 years—Reuters[5]*
*The U.S. economy is on a tear—Wall Street Journal[6]*

Half of our nation, by all reasonable estimates of human need, is in or near poverty.[7] The jubilant headlines above speak for people whose view is distorted by growing financial wealth. The argument for a barely surviving half of America has been made before, but new data keeps appearing to strengthen the case, and more and more Americans are becoming *disposable*,[8] recognized as either commodities or criminals by the more fortunate members of society. There seems to be a method to the madness of winner-take-all capitalism. The following steps, whether due to greed, indifference, or disdain, are the means by which America's wealth-takers dispose of the people they don't need.

## 1. Deplete Their Wealth

The bottom half of America relies primarily on housing for its share of wealth. But middle-class housing, which just 35 years ago was about *seven times the value* of total investment wealth for the 12,000 richest families (0.01 percent), was by 2014 only worth half of that investment wealth.[9] Since the recession, median wealth dropped a stunning 40 percent, leaving the poorest half with negative net worth.[10] Debt has decimated their remaining wealth. Emmanuel Saez and Gabriel Zucman summarize: "The bottom half of the distribution always owns close to zero wealth on net. Hence, the bottom 90% wealth share is the same as the share of wealth owned by top 50–90% families—what can be described as the middle class."[11]

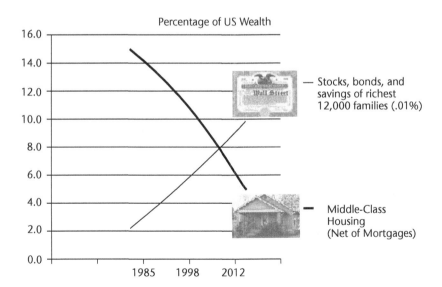

**FIGURE 4.4** Wealth: Stocks vs. Housing (based on author's analysis).
(www.commondreams.org/views/2014/12/01/slap-face-wealth-gap-images)
(http://gabriel-zucman.eu/files/SaezZucman2014.pdf, Figure 8)
(www.levyinstitute.org/pubs/wp_589.pdf, Table 3).

Ample evidence exists to show that half of America is in or near poverty. Pew Research revealed that half of American households spend more than they earn.[12] A Bankrate study found that 62 percent of Americans are unable to afford a $500 brake job with cash from their savings.[13] A Federal Reserve survey found that nearly half of respondents could not cover a $400 emergency expense.[14] According to a study by Go Banking Rates, nearly 50 percent of Americans have no savings, and over 70 percent of us have less than $1,000.

## 2. Strip Away Their Income

This chart from Pew Research[15] shows the dramatic shrinking of the middle class, defined as "adults whose annual household income is two-thirds to double the national median, about $42,000 to $126,000 annually in 2014 dollars." Evidence keeps accumulating.[16] A National Bureau of Economic Research report refers to it as a "hollowing out" of the middle class.[17]

In 1970, according to Pew, *three of every ten* income dollars went to upper-income households. Now, *five of every ten* dollars goes to them.[18]

Market watchers rave about "bright" and "blockbuster" jobs reports.[19] But any upbeat news about the unemployment rate must be balanced against the fact that nine of the ten fastest growing occupations don't require a college degree. Jobs gained since the recession are paying 23 percent less than jobs lost.[20] Low-wage jobs (up to $13.33 per hour) made up just 22 percent of the jobs lost to the recession, but accounted for 44 percent of the jobs regained during the first four years of the recovery.[21] Worsening the situation is the recent finding that the U.S. is last among developed countries in workplace benefits such as maternity leave and sick pay.[22]

**Share of adults living in middle-income households is falling**

% of adults in each income tier

| | Lowest | Lower middle | Middle | Upper middle | Highest |
|---|---|---|---|---|---|
| 2015 | 20 | 9 | 50 | 12 | 9 |
| 2011 | 20 | 9 | 51 | 12 | 8 |
| 2001 | 18 | 9 | 54 | 11 | 7 |
| 1991 | 18 | 9 | 56 | 12 | 6 |
| 1981 | 17 | 9 | 59 | 12 | 3 |
| 1971 | 16 | 9 | 61 | 10 | 4 |

Note: Adults are assigned to income tiers based on their size-adjusted household income in the calendar year prior to the survey year. Figures may not add to 100% due to rounding.

Source: Pew Research Center analysis of the Current Population Survey, Annual Social and Economic Supplements

PEW RESEARCH CENTER

**FIGURE 4.5** "The American Middle Class is Losing Ground."
Pew Research, December 9, 2015 (www.pewsocialtrends.org/2015/12/09/the-american-middle-class-is-losing-ground/).

Furthermore, the official 5 percent unemployment rate is actually 10 percent when part-time and discouraged (no longer looking) workers are included.[23] It's very likely higher. People are falling fast from the ranks of middle-class living.

Hourly wages have been stagnant for over 40 years. Productivity has grown 72 percent since 1973, while median hourly compensation rose just 8.7 percent.[24] Earnings due to workers for their years of productivity have gone to already-rich people.[25] In the first three years after the 2008–9 recession, the richest one percent took up to 116 percent of the new income gains after the recession. Yes, 116 percent, because almost everyone else went backwards.[26]

According to the Social Security Administration,[27] over half of Americans make less than $30,000 per year. That's less than the median national living wage of $16.87 per hour, as calculated by Alliance for a Just Society (AJS), and it's not enough—*even with two full-time workers*—to attain an "adequate but modest living standard" for a family of four, which at the median is over $60,000, according to the Economic Policy Institute.[28]

AJS found that there are *seven job seekers for every job opening* that pays enough ($15 per hour) for a single adult to make ends meet.[29]

## 3. Take Away Their Homes

A study by the National Low Income Housing Coalition[30] concluded that an average American renter would need to earn $18.92 per hour—over twice the minimum wage—to afford a two-bedroom apartment. "In no state," their report says, "can a full-time minimum wage worker afford a one-bedroom or a two-bedroom rental unit at Fair Market Rent." Over one-eighth of the nation's supply of low-income housing has been permanently lost since 2001.[31] The number of families spending more than half their incomes on rent—the 'severely' cost-burdened renters—has surged from 7.5 million to 11.4 million in the last decade, over a 50 percent increase.[32] Yet plenty of accommodation is available for those who can pay, for it is estimated that *for each homeless person* (over 600,000 on any January night) *up to 29 homes or apartments are sitting vacant* around the country, waiting to fetch a big profit for their owners and landlords.[33]

In Milwaukee, where author Matthew Desmond lived among the poor for nearly a year to experience the effects of the affordable housing crisis, *eviction* is common, especially for single mothers, who are paying up to 70 percent of their income on rent and electricity. Says Desmond, "Poor black men were locked up. Poor black women were locked out."[34]

In New Orleans, tens of thousands of African-Americans have been forced to leave the city as starry-eyed developers have more than doubled the rents to attract the wealthy.[35] Louisiana Republican Richard H. Baker thanked God for the change: "We finally cleaned up public housing in New Orleans. We couldn't do it. But God did."

As for single-family homes, Trulia has reported that the number of starter homes (bottom third by price) available in the hundred largest U.S. cities has dropped by about 44 percent in the past four years. The median price of a starter home in San Francisco is a staggering $700,000. In other major metropolitan areas, it ranges between $200,000 and $400,000, with about half of a family's income needed to afford a purchase.[36]

Blackstone and Goldman Sachs are masters at the housing game, with three relentlessly effective strategies:[37]

1. Buy houses and hold them to force prices up.
2. Charge high rents (with minimal maintenance).
3. Package the deals as rental-backed securities with artificially high-grade ratings.

## 4. Take Away Their Sustenance

- The Koch-funded Cato Institute contends: *SNAP helps breed dependency and undermines the work ethic.*[38]
- The Heritage Foundation, also Koch-funded, condescends: *Helping the poor should mean promoting individual freedom through self-reliance.*[39]
- No jobs? No problem, says Eric Cantor (R-Virginia), *You could go and participate in community service activities or a workfare program.*

In reality, community centers are not all that receptive to walk-in applicants.

Poor families don't want handouts. As noted earlier, nearly two-thirds of all working-age poor are actually working. But unable to earn a living wage, they have to rely on food stamps, which only provide about $5 a day for meals.[40]

Food stamp opponents should consider the fact that nearly half the recipients are children.[41] Before the recession, 12 out of every 100 American children got food stamps. After the recession, 20 out of every 100 American children got food stamps. That's nearly a 70 percent increase, from 9.5 million children in 2007 to 16 million in 2014, at the same time that U.S. wealth was growing by over $30 trillion. Even with that incomprehensible increase in wealth, our nation was not able to ensure food security for millions of its most vulnerable citizens.[42]

## 5. Fleece Them with Fines and Fees

The poor half of America is victimized by the banking industry, which takes an average of $2,412 each year from underserved households for interest and fees on alternative financial services;[43] by rental centers that charge effective annual interest rates over 100 percent; by payday lenders who charge effective annual interest rates of over 1,000 percent;[44] and by the burgeoning prison industry, which charges prisoners for food, health care, phone calls, probation monitoring, and anything else they can think of.

On top of all this, bubbly TV personalities rave about all the lottery money just waiting to be taken home. They say little about the almost nonexistent chances of hitting it big. As a result of the hype and their lack of awareness, poor households have been estimated to spend anywhere from five to nine percent of their earnings on lotteries.[45]

## 6. Criminalize Them

In a survey of 187 cities, the National Law Center on Homelessness & Poverty found that 18 percent of cities impose bans on sleeping in public, 53 percent of cities prohibit sitting in particular public places, and 9 percent of cities prohibit sharing food with homeless people.[46]

The homeless are feared by the upper classes, and they're often arrested for nonexistent or nonviolent infractions, in good part because they are simply considered "offensive" to people of means. They usually have personal problems that society has failed to address. A study of nearly 50,000 cases revealed that most deal with alcohol or drug abuse, and with mental health issues.[47]

Legislating against impoverished people is expensive: shelters, emergency rooms, jail cells. The Interagency Council on Homelessness estimates the cost at between $30,000 and $50,000 per person per year.[48] In Utah and Arizona, a program called Housing First has cut costs dramatically by providing apartments to the homeless, with no strings attached, and similar positive results were experienced in programs in New York City and Seattle. Once-penniless people thrived in their own homes, acting responsibly, improving their lives, harming no one, and all at a cost saving for the local community.[49]

## 7. Insult Them

The Charles Koch Foundation recently released a commercial that ranked a near-poverty-level $34,000 family among the top one percent in the world.[50] Bud Konheim, CEO and co-founder of fashion company Nicole Miller, concurred: "The guy that's making, oh my God, he's making $35,000 a year, why don't we try that out in India or some countries we can't even name. China, anyplace, the guy is wealthy."[51]

Another affront comes from libertarian Charles Murray,[52] who wrote: "There remains a core of civic virtue and involvement in working-class America... Married, educated people who work hard and conscientiously raise their kids shouldn't hesitate to voice their disapproval of those who defy these norms." Senator Marco Rubio agrees, calling marriage the "greatest tool" for lifting families out of poverty.

Here are the facts: Upper-class and lower-class divorce rates rose and fell in similar fashion until the late 1980s, around the time inequality began to rip apart the fabric of American society, and to break down low-income family life. Studies show that children whose families receive housing vouchers end up with higher marriage rates.[53] And despite what Murray's followers might think, race isn't a factor. As noted earlier, Pew Research[54] and the Centers for Disease Control found little difference between white and black fathers in the nature or extent of their relationships with their children.[55]

## 8. Hope That They Just Go Away

An "emergency financial manager" (EFM) privatizes the democratic process, stripping citizens and elected officials of power, granting unlimited power to a CEO-like figure who can sell off public assets to save money, even when it threatens the people of the community.

Most of the democracy-killing EFM schemes in the State of Michigan have been directed toward poor black communities. The one in Flint,[56] which imposed a cost-cutting measure leading to the poisoning of the city's children, may be the most egregious example of disdain for low-income minorities. As writer Dave Johnson explains, "Government in a democracy is nothing like a business. It is supposed to organize itself to deliver services and make people's lives better, not profit off the people."[57]

In the grimmest form of irony, Flint residents were paying some of the highest water rates in their Michigan county. They were threatened with a shutdown of water[58] (still needed for toilets and cleaning) if they didn't keep paying for the toxic product. With yet another suggestion of inhumanity, undocumented immigrants in Flint were unable to acquire free water because of their fear of the authorities at government water disbursement centers.

## Evidence That Poor People Aren't Lazy[59]

Many wealthy white conservative males believe they deserve their good fortunes, and that the poor are taking handouts.[60] But on average, little of the money of the wealthiest Americans is spent on productive job-creating ventures. Potential young entrepreneurs, in contrast, are too often mired in debt and deprived of opportunities to prosper.

Based on the evidence, the very people demeaned by the rich as "lazy" are generally the hardest workers.

## Most Safety Net Recipients Are Working

Almost 63 percent of America's work-eligible poor are working, and 73 percent of public support recipients are members of working families.[61] Over 83 percent of all benefits going to low-income people are for the elderly, the disabled, or working households. As noted by Paul Krugman, "only 26 percent of jobless Americans are receiving any kind of unemployment benefit, the lowest level in many decades."

And the money is used for the intended need: the USDA estimates that only one cent of every food stamp dollar is used in a fraudulent manner.[62]

## For Those Who Aren't Working, Living-Wage Opportunities Aren't Available

Congress has continually thwarted job creation proposals, contributing to a stunning increase in the long-term unemployment rate, from 17.5 percent to 43.7 percent after the recession, and then down to a still-middle-class-crushing 27 percent today.[63]

## Middle Class Has Produced the Entrepreneurs. Until Recently.

Experience has shown that productive new ideas, and the job creation that comes with them, have traditionally been generated by young middle-class people.[64] But as debt and job loss has plagued this part of America over the past 30 years, the number of new startups has dropped dramatically.[65] Today, the percentage of wealth derived from entrepreneurship in America is only about half the world's average, as more and more wealth comes from stocks, real estate, and inheritance.[66] With the drop-off in middle-class risk-taking, entrepreneurial enterprises are increasingly being initiated by people who already have money or connections with established businesses.[67]

## Immigrants Bring Entrepreneurship

According to the *Wall Street Journal*, immigrants make up 13 percent of the population, but 28 percent of the small business owners.[68] A recent study found that immigrants started ***more than half*** of current U.S. startups valued at $1 billion or more.[69] Plus, they boost local economies by starting businesses in developing neighborhoods. In the last three years, the number of Hispanic-owned businesses has grown at an annual rate 15 times that of the rate for all companies.[70]

## Income Experiments Show that the Poor Use Money Productively

Results from a 2005 program in Britain support the argument that the reduction of poverty promotes family stability, rather than the other way around.[71] Increases in family income, especially through work opportunities, led to "sharp and sustained decreases in material hardship for the most vulnerable families," and, in the cases of households with children, more spending on family needs and less on alcohol and tobacco. A broader study of 18 European countries found "increasing employment commitment as social spending gets more generous"—in other words, dividend payments encourage people to work harder, rather than to waste the money.[72]

## At the Other Extreme: The Idle Rich

For every ONE DOLLAR in safety net programs, SIX DOLLARS goes to tax expenditures, tax underpayments, tax havens, and corporate nonpayment. The very rich get the handouts; in most cases, the hardest workers are those who have to fight their way up from the bottom.[73]

## Us Against the World

The U.S. is the only region in the world where the middle class does not own its equivalent share of wealth. The North American middle class, as defined in 2015 by Credit Suisse, and of which the U.S. is by far the largest part, has 39 percent of the people but only 21 percent of national wealth. Every other region of the world shows the reverse phenomenon, with the middle class owning an oversized portion of national wealth.

The Credit Suisse Global Wealth Report states: "The average wealth of middle-class adults in North America is barely half the average for all adults. In contrast, middle-class wealth per adult in Europe is 130% of the regional average; the middle class in China is three times better off in wealth terms than the country as a whole; and the average wealth of the middle class in both India and Africa is ten times the level of those in the rest of the population."[74]

Two-thirds of Americans own only about 7 percent of our country's wealth, compared to an ownership of 13 percent or more for a comparable group in all other reporting nations.

## The Poor, Personally

Melissa Mays,[75] a resident of Flint, Michigan, noticed a change in the color and odor of her tap water. Soon afterwards, she developed a rash and clumps of her hair began to fall out. Her family now spends nearly $400 a month on bottled water. Another Flint resident, Bethany Hazard, called the city to report the sewer-like odor of the brownish water, but she was told there was nothing to worry about. Resident LeeAnne Walters watched her children develop rashes on their arms and legs. Her 14-year-old son missed a month of school. When she sent a sample of the water to a professor of environmental studies, a shocking result was returned: lead content of 13,000 parts per billion, compared to the Environmental Protection Agency danger level of 15 parts per billion.

Diedre Melson[76] was making $13.52 an hour at a non-profit that referred low-income people to social service programs. But she couldn't support her family on that near-median wage and had to turn to food stamps, like many of the people she served. Others have it much worse. Lissette Vega[77] left a wife-beating husband, took her baby with her, found a $9 per hour job, but couldn't find an affordable apartment. She became homeless. Daphna Browne suffered from depression, but still managed to maintain a $650 per month apartment in New York City for herself and her 10-year-old daughter. But she was evicted, because the landlord could rent the apartment for more money. Marcia,[78] a 56-year-old homeless woman in San Francisco, spoke about the shame and misery of walking the streets: "Saturdays and Sundays are hell for those of us who are homeless, because most walk-in centers are closed. I especially hate Sundays. That's when I ride [the subway]." Or the bus. Said another homeless woman, "If you don't get a nice driver, you have to get off every hour or so and wait for another one. If you have to wait for a bus at three in the morning, you'll be waiting a long time. Anything can happen."

The Center for Effective Government[79] has collected stories of Americans, many of them well-educated with ample work experience, who have struggled to maintain even minimal standards of living for their families.

- From Lerna, Illinois: *I was teaching high school biology until I was laid off...We are already running out of things to eat...After a lifetime of dedicating ourselves to the welfare of the nation's children, must we be taken apart and thrown into the street? We are scared.*
- From Basking Ridge, New Jersey: *I have submitted over 300 resumes and cover letters to many different types of industries...I have exhausted all of my savings...*
- From Castle Rock, Colorado: *All of my reserves are gone and I cannot support my daughter as a single parent...I am older, 49, have a master's degree and many years of excellent experience, but no one will hire me...I have been told by interviewers on multiple occasions that I have an impressive resume...*
- From Hampton, Virginia: *I am a disabled veteran who was working for the U.S. Army as a contractor for four years...It is really hard as someone who was cut from a job to hear [politicians] call the working people lazy...*

Most families have kids to provide for.

- From Dallas, Texas: *I have kids who are 14 and 13. I don't want to lose them to the streets.*
- From Orange, California: *I have two small children and a wife who is partially disabled and works part time. We lost our house and now all live in a studio apartment.*
- From Massachusetts: *I was just informed the foreclosure process on my home is going to begin. I am a single mother, and I have nowhere to go but a shelter. I cannot believe I live in America.*

A *60 Minutes* report[80] detailed some of the day-to-day struggles of the family of 11-year-old Destiny Corfee, who told the TV correspondent, "I never really noticed what people were actually going through until now; until we're actually going through it too."

Destiny's parents, David and Theresa, had recently owned a three-bedroom home, and they had supported the family with a prosperous auto-detailing business. But they lost their jobs and they lost the house. Rather than risk splitting up the family, they loaded their three kids into their van and parked it at a Walmart, which for a time would serve as the family bathroom. Said Destiny's brother: "We would actually go in Walmart and clean our self up before we'd go to school...I would like wash my face, and like, take a tissue and wash my arms and stuff...We would bring the toothpaste and the toothbrush and the brushes so we'll go brush our hair in the mirror...And it would be kind of weird."

After David found employment as a day laborer, the family moved to a hotel room. Most of their possessions were put in storage, and subsequently forfeited when the bill couldn't be paid. Items important to the children were never to be seen again: a scooter, a video game system, Barbie dolls. More importantly, the hotel was in a run-down part of town. Destiny had heard about nearby shootings.

When it became apparent that day labor wouldn't be enough to keep the hotel room and feed the kids, David hatched a new plan. "As embarrassing as it was, I sat down with a magic marker, and...I wrote a sign out. It said, 'Please help, family of five.' Every truck that went by I would holler out to them, and let them see my sign. 'Hey, do you need any help? Can I get a job? Do you need any help?'" Destiny was embarrassed. "I don't want people to know that...he's my dad."

But her father was realistic, and determined, hiding his own embarrassment to provide for the family. "Never and in a million years did I think that that would be me. And I told my wife, 'This is America. And America is full of wonderful people. And I'm gonna go out and see what I can do and see if there's someone out there that can help us.'" After a while, he found a job as a parking attendant, for $10 an hour.

The *60 Minutes* correspondent received a variety of responses when he asked young Florida students, some of them homeless, what it's like to feel hungry. "It's hard," said one. "You can't sleep. You just wait, you just go to sleep for like five minutes and you wake up again. And your stomach hurts."

For many of their families, a choice had to be made between food and electricity. When the kids were asked how many had the lights turned off in their homes, most of them raised their hands.

## Notes

1 "Massive Dust Storm Sweeps South Dakota." *This Day in History*, History.com; "About the Dust Bowl." University of Illinois; "Surviving the Dust Bowl." *American Experience*, Public Broadcasting System.
2 "Global Wealth Databook." Credit Suisse, 2016.

3 Buchheit, Paul, "The 6-Step Process to Wipe Out the Poor Half of America." CommonDreams.org, December 15, 2014.

4 Long, Heather, "Happy Monday! S&P 500 now up 10% for year." CNN Money, November 10, 2014.

5 Mutikani, Lucia, "Third-quarter U.S. economic growth strongest in 11 years." Reuters, December 23, 2014.

6 King, Neil, "The Upbeat Economy Spurs a Political Fight for Credit, but Little Else." *Wall Street Journal*, January 9, 2015.

7 Buchheit, Paul, "More Evidence that Half of America Is in or near Poverty." NationOfChange.org, March 24, 2014.

8 Giroux, Henry A., *Disposable Youth: Racialized Memories, and the Culture of Cruelty.* Routledge, 2012.

9 Buchheit, Paul, "Slap-in-the-Face Wealth Gap Images." CommonDreams.org, December 1, 2014.

10 Wolff, Edward N., "Household Wealth Trends in the United States, 1962–2013." National Bureau of Economic Research, 2014.

11 Saez, Emmanuel and Zucman, Gabriel, "Wealth Inequality in the United States Since 1913." National Bureau of Economic Research, October, 2014.

12 "The Precarious State of Family Balance Sheets." The Pew Charitable Trusts, January, 2015.

13 Bell, Claes, "Budgets Can Crumble in Times of Trouble." Bankrate.com, January, 2015.

14 "Report on the Economic Well-Being of U.S. Households in 2014." The Federal Reserve, May, 2015.

15 "The American Middle Class is Losing Ground." Pew Research Center, December 9, 2015.

16 "America's Shrinking Middle Class: A Close Look at Changes within Metropolitan Areas." Pew Research Center, May 11, 2016.

17 Komlos, John, "Growth of Income and Welfare in the U.S., 1979–2011." National Bureau of Economic Research, April, 2016.

18 "The American Middle Class is Losing Ground." Op. cit.

19 "7 Charts Show how Friday's Amazing Jobs Report Rocked the Market." *MarketWatch*, November 6, 2015.

20 "Income and Wage Gaps Across the US." The United States Conference of Mayors, August, 2014.

21 "The Low-Wage Recovery." National Employment Law Project, April 2014.

22 Van Amburg, Jessie, "U.S. Has Least Generous Benefits of Western Nations, Study Says." Time.com, February 17, 2016.

23 Bureau of Labor Statistics, 2016 (www.bls.gov/news.release/empsit.t15.htm), accessed September 1, 2015.

24 Bivens, Josh and Mishel, Lawrence, "Understanding the Historic Divergence Between Productivity and a Typical Worker's Pay." Economic Policy Institute, September 2, 2015.

25 Saez, Emmanuel, "Striking it Richer: The Evolution of Top Incomes in the United States." UC Berkeley, June 25, 2015.

26 Tcherneva, Pavlina, "Growth for Whom?" Levy Economics Institute, October 6, 2014.

27 "Wage Statistics for 2014." Social Security Administration, February 24, 2016.

28 "What Families Need to Get by." Economic Policy Institute, July 3, 2013.

29 Fredericksen, Allyson, "Patchwork of Paychecks." Alliance for a Just Society, December 2015.

30 "Out of Reach 2014." National Low Income Housing Coalition, 2016.

31 "No Safe Place: The Criminalization of Homelessness in U.S. Cities." National Law Center on Homelessness & Poverty, 2014.

32 Olick, Diana, "Housing's New Crisis: Half Your Income for Rent." CNBC, December 9, 2015.

33 Larson, Rob, "The 1 Percent's Houses Are Getting Bigger and Swankier while Average Americans Struggle to Make Rent." *In These Times*, September 23, 2015.

34 Desmond, Matthew, *Evicted: Poverty and Profit in the American City*. Crown Publishers, 2016.

35 Adams, Thomas Jessen, "How the Ruling Class Remade New Orleans." *Portside*, August 30, 2015.

36 Badger, Emily, "Why it Seems Impossible to Buy Your First Home." *Washington Post*, March 22, 2016.

37 Perlberg, Heather and Gittelsohn, John, "Wall Street Unlocks Profits from Distress with Rental Revolution." *Bloomberg*, December 19, 2013; Goldstein, Matthew; Ablan, Jennifer; Tara LaCapra, Lauren: "Exclusive: Ex-Goldman Mortgage Chief Plans Foreclosed Home Fund." Reuters, July 19, 2012.

38 Tanner, Michael D., "SNAP Theatrics Fall Flat." From *National Review* (Online), June 26, 2013.

39 Sheffield, Rachel, "Food Stamp Participation the Highest Ever...and Growing." *Daily Signal*, April 23, 2012.

40 Budget Summary. U.S. Department of Agriculture, 2015.

41 "Fact vs. Fiction: USDA's Supplemental Nutrition Assistance Program." U.S. Dept. of Agriculture, June 24, 2011.

42 Cohn, Emily, "One in 5 American Kids Are On Food Stamps." *Huffington Post*, January 28, 2015.

43 "Providing Non-Bank Financial Services for the Underserved." US Postal Service, January 27, 2014.

44 Singletary, Michelle, "The Trap of Payday Loans can Lead to Triple-Digit Interest Rates." *Washington Post*, March 25, 2014.

45 Williams, Geoff, "Poor People Spend 9% of Income on Lottery Tickets; Here's Why." *Daily Finance*, May 31, 2010.

46 National Law Center on Homelessness & Poverty, Op. cit.

47 Fitzpatrick, Kevin M. and Myrstol, Brad. "The Jailing of America's Homeless: Evaluating the Rabble Management Thesis." *Crime & Delinquency*, 2011.

48 "People Experiencing Chronic Homelessness." Interagency Council on Homelessness, updated 2016.

49 Sanburn, Josh, "The Radically Simple Solution to Homelessness." *Time*, March 3, 2016.

50 "Economic Freedom in 60 Seconds." Charles Koch Foundation (www.youtube.com/watch?v=gpLfQvRmf2E&feature=youtu.be), accessed October 1, 2016.

51 Frank, Robert, "Luxury CEO: The Poor Should Stop Whining." CNBC, February 12, 2014.

52 Murray, Charles, "The New American Divide." *The Wall Street Journal*, January 21, 2012.

53 "Groundbreaking Studies: Good Neighborhoods Help Low-Income Children Succeed." Center on Budget and Policy Priorities, May 4, 2015.

54 "The New American Father." Pew Research Center, June 14, 2013.

55 "Fathers' Involvement with Their Children." *National Health Statistics Report*, December 20, 2013.

56 "Documentary: Undrinkable—Flint, Michigan—Poisoned Water." DTV News, January 8, 2016.

57 Johnson, Dave, "Government Run Like a Business Led to Lead in Flint's Water." NationOfChange.org, January 21, 2016.

58 "The State of Public Water in the United States." Food & Water Watch, foodandwaterwatch.org.

59 Buchheit, Paul, "Evidence That Poor People Aren't Lazy." CommonDreams.org, November 30, 2015.

60 Phillips, L. Taylor and Lowery, Brian S., "The Hard-Knock Life? Whites Claim Hardships in Response to Racial Inequity." *Journal of Experimental Social Psychology*, November 2015.

61 Gould, Elise, "Poor People Work: A Majority of Poor People Who Can Work Do." Economic Policy Institute, May 19, 2015; Jacobs, Ken; Perry, Ian; MacGillvary, Jenifer: "The High Public Cost of Low Wages." UC Berkeley Center for Labor Research and Education, April 2015.

62 "What is SNAP Fraud?" US Dept. of Agriculture, April 2014.

63 Bureau of Labor Statistics (www.bls.gov/news.release/empsit.t12.htm), accessed November 14, 2016.

64 Boushey, Heather and Hersh, Adam S., "The American Middle Class, Income Inequality, and the Strength of Our Economy: New Evidence in Economics." *Center for American Progress*, May 2012.

65 Thompson, Derek, "The Myth of the Millennial Entrepreneur." *The Atlantic*, July 6, 2016; Lowrey, Annie, "Don't Let the Disruption Hype Fool You: America is Actually Getting Less Entrepreneurial." *New York News & Politics*, August 5, 2014.

66 "A Changing Wealth Landscape." Barclays, 2016.

67 Groth, Aimee, "Entrepreneurs Don't Have a Special Gene for Risk—They Come from Families with Money." *Quartz*, July 17, 2015.

68 "Immigrant Entrepreneurs Prosper on Main Street." *The Wall Street Journal*, January 13, 2015.

69 Koh, Yoree, "Study: Immigrants Founded 51% of U.S. Billion-Dollar Startups." *Wall Street Journal*, March 17, 2016.

70 Rosenberg, Joyce M., "Get Started: Hispanic Business Growth Outstrips Rest of US." AP, September 21, 2015.

71 Waldfogel, Jane, "Tackling Child Poverty and Improving Child Well-Being." Foundation for Child Development, December 2010.

72  van der Wel, Kjetil A. and Halvorsen, Knut, "The Bigger the Worse? A Comparative Study of the Welfare State and Employment Commitment." Sage: *Work, Employment, and Society*, February 2, 2015.

73  Buchheit, Paul, "Why So Many Americans Defend the Failed Capitalist Experiment." CommonDreams.org, September 14, 2015.

74  "Global Wealth Databook." Credit Suisse, 2015.

75  Smith, Mitch, "A Water Dilemma in Michigan. Cloudy or Costly?" *New York Times*, March 24, 2015.

76  Yurechko, Jane, "Struggling Workers Assess The 'American Dream': It's Still Economic Winter." Campaign for America's Future, June 7, 2013.

77  Bader, Eleanor J., "Gimme Shelter: Government Policies Fail Homeless Mothers and Kids." Truthout.org, November 3, 2012.

78  Aguilar, Rose, "Old, Female and Homeless." *The Nation*, January 30, 2013.

79  Center for Effective Government (www.foreffectivegov.org/reports/), accessed November 14, 2016.

80  Pelley, Scott, Reporter: "Homeless Children: the Hard Times Generation." *60 Minutes*, CBS News, June 20, 2011.

## Bibliography

Desmond, Matthew, *Evicted: Poverty and Profit in the American City*. Crown Publishers, 2016.

Frank, Robert H., *Falling Behind: How Rising Inequality Harms the Middle Class*. University of California Press, 2007.

Hulme, David and Wilkinson, Rorden (Editors), *Routledge Handbook of Global Poverty and Inequality*. Routledge, 2016.

Page, Benjamin and Jacobs, Lawrence, *Class War? What Americans Really Think about Economic Inequality*. University of Chicago Press, 2009.

Wise, Tim, *Under the Affluence: Shaming the Poor, Praising the Rich and Sacrificing the Future of America*. City Lights Open Media, 2015.

Wysong, Earl; Perrucci, Robert; and Wright, David: *The New Class Society: Goodbye American Dream?* Rowman & Littlefield, fourth edition, 2014.

# 5

# EVERYONE DESERVES AN INCOME

The majority (57 percent) of **basic research**, the essential startup work for products that don't yet yield profits, is paid for by our tax dollars. When ALL forms of research are included—basic, applied, and developmental—approximately 30 percent comes from public money. In 2009, universities were still receiving ten times more science and engineering funding from government than from industry.[1]

To the daydreamers, Steve Jobs started with boxes of silicon and wires in a garage and fashioned the first iPhone. The reality is explained by Mariana Mazzucato:[2] "Everything you can do with an iPhone was government-funded. From the Internet that allows you to surf the Web, to GPS that lets you use Google Maps, to touchscreen display and even the SIRI voice activated system—all of these things were funded by Uncle Sam through the Defense Advanced Research Projects Agency (DARPA), NASA, the Navy, and even the CIA."

**All the technology** in our phones and computers started with government research at the Defense Department, the National Science Foundation, the Census Bureau, and public universities. The internet made possible the quadrillion-dollar trading capacity of the financial industry. Google is using some of its billions to **buy technologies that were built by DARPA with our tax money**. Pharmaceutical companies wouldn't exist without funding from the taxpayers, who have provided support for decades through the National Institutes of Health,[3] and who still pay over 80 percent of the cost of basic research for new drugs and vaccines. As Ralph Nader notes, "The pharmaceutical industry receives billions of dollars in tax credits for doing research and development that it should be doing anyway."

There's much more. The wealthiest individuals and corporations are the main beneficiaries of tax laws, tax breaks, property rights, zoning rules, copyright provisions, trade pacts, antitrust legislation, and contract regulations. Pharmaceutical companies claim patents on medications that were developed through many years of government research and development. The largest companies also benefit, despite their publicly voiced objections to regulatory agencies, from SBA and SEC guidelines that generally favor business, and from FDA and USDA quality-control measures that minimize consumer complaints and product recalls.

Businesses rely on roads, seaports, and airports to ship their products, the FAA, TSA, Coast Guard and Department of Transportation to safeguard them, a nationwide energy grid to power their factories, communications towers and satellites to conduct online business, the Department of Commerce to promote and safeguard global markets, the U.S. Navy to monitor shipping lanes, and FEMA to clean up after them. Thanks to the taxpayer-funded National Highway System, corporations like Fedex and United Parcel have access to markets across the country. Along with road construction come the water, electric, and telephone facilities needed to sustain big business.

The richest individuals and corporations are also the primary beneficiaries of the $60 billion spent on Homeland Security.[4]

And they get free rein to pollute our homeland, at almost no cost. A century-and-a-half-old mining law allows companies to exploit the environment, pollute land and water, and escape public oversight, all while paying little or no royalties. As oil companies despoil our waterways, management writes off fines as a cost of doing business. Said BP's Laura Folse: "I personally have no concern about oil washing in from the offshore to the shoreline."[5]

For international business, more advantages are enjoyed by multinational corporations through trade agreements like NAFTA, with international disputes resolved by the business-friendly World Bank, International Monetary Fund, and World Trade Organization. Federal judicial law protects our biggest companies from foreign infringement. The proposed Trans-Pacific Partnership would put governments around the world at the mercy of corporate decision makers.

## A Note on Philanthrocapitalism[6]

We as a nation have failed to find a way to ensure that everyone has the *opportunity* to benefit from our steadily accumulating wealth. Instead, we are turning more and more to private money, to individuals who are viewed as society's benefactors, surrogates for disappearing tax sources, funders of essential services for the future. But there is little incentive for them to support the very people who would most benefit from a guaranteed income. As Robert Reich notes, about two-thirds of "charitable" donations from the rich go to their foundations and alma maters, and to "culture palaces"—operas, art museums, symphonies, and theaters.

On a global scale, one need only consider health care, where it has been estimated that less than 10 percent of the budget for health research is spent on diseases that cause 90 percent of the world's illnesses. And according to a study in *The Lancet*, only four of the 336 new drugs developed in the first decade of this century were for diseases impacting low-income people.[7]

As World Health Organization Director Margaret Chan explained about the Ebola virus: "Ebola has historically been confined to poor African nations. The R&D incentive is virtually non-existent. A profit-driven industry does not invest in products for markets that cannot pay."[8]

The rise of "philanthrocapitalism"[9] has allowed tech titans like Mark Zuckerberg and Bill Gates, along with hedge fund and private equity billionaires, to reduce their taxes—thus depriving society of infrastructure and education funds—while they assume the right to make high-level decisions about GMO agriculture, charter schools, and internet usage.[10] They preempt the democratic process while offering little transparency for their actions. Much of their funding goes to corporate partners that do the bidding of their billionaire benefactors. Some of it even goes to companies whose philanthropic interests conflict with those of society as a whole. Zuckerberg's foundation is structured as a for-profit corporation, an LLC, which will have many of the benefits of a charity while operating as a business.[11] The Gates Foundation partners with Coca-Cola, and has extensive holdings in oil companies, while both Gates and Zuckerberg have connections with Monsanto.[12] Some experts believe that the Gates Foundation's support of corporate patent protection has helped to stifle competition with the generic pharmaceutical companies that might otherwise provide low-cost drugs to the global market.[13]

The Global Justice report "Gated Development"[14] describes the role of the Bill & Melinda Gates Foundation (BMGF) as "deepening...the role of multinational companies in global health and agriculture especially, even though these corporations are responsible for much of the poverty and injustice that already plagues the global south." The report notes that "the BMGF is a private US foundation, and remains unaccountable to public bodies...Even worse, the BMGF appears to have bought the silence of academics, NGOs and the media who might otherwise be expected to criticise aspects of the foundation's work."

## Notes

1 "Universities Report $55 Billion in Science and Engineering R&D Spending for FY 2009." National Science Foundation, September 2010.

2 Mazzucato, Mariana, *The Entrepreneurial State: Debunking Public vs. Private Sector Myths.* Anthem Press, 2013.

3 Mazzucato, Mariana, "How Taxpayers Prop up Big Pharma, and How to Cap That." *The Los Angeles Times*, October 27, 2015.

4 "Budget-in-Brief: Fiscal Year 2016." Dept. of Homeland Security.

5 "11 Memorable Quotes from the BP Oil Spill Trial's Final Phase." *New Orleans Times-Picayune*, February 11, 2015 (www.nola.com/business/index.ssf/2015/02/11_memorable_quotes_from_the_b.html#7).

6 Saltman, Kenneth J., *The Gift of Education: Public Education and Venture Philanthropy (Education, Politics and Public Life).* Palgrave Macmillan, 2010.

7 "The Drug and Vaccine Landscape for Neglected Diseases (2000–11): A Systematic Assessment." *The Lancet*, October 24, 2013.

8 "WHO Director-General Addresses the Regional Committee for Africa." World Health Organization, November 3, 2014.

9 McGoey, Linsey, *No Such Thing as a Free Gift: The Gates Foundation and the Price of Philanthropy*. Verso, 2015.

10 MacGillis, Alec, "The Billionaires' Loophole." *The New Yorker*, March 14, 2016.

11 Barkan, Joanne, "Wealthy Philanthropists Shouldn't Impose Their Idea of Common Good on Us." *The Guardian*, December 3, 2015.

12 McGoey, Linsey, "No Such Thing as a Free Gift: The Gates Foundation and the Price of Philanthropy." Verso, 2016 (www.truth-out.org/progressivepicks/item/34321-beware-of-philanthro-capitalists-bearing-gifts), accessed November 14, 2016.

13 Shiva, Vandana, "'Free Basics' Will Take Away More Than Our Right to the Internet." Common Dreams, December 29, 2015 (http://commondreams.org/views/2015/12/29/free-basics-will-take-away-more-our-right-internet), accessed November 14, 2016.

14 "Gated Development—Is the Gates Foundation Always a Force for Good?" *Global Justice*, January 2016.

# 6

# AFRICAN-AMERICANS

American minorities have been subjugated in varying degrees to the interests of profit-making.[1] Native American civilizations were wiped out; Mexicans owned California, then were violently turned away during the Gold Rush; the Chinese cut through mountains to build our railroads, then faced the Chinese Exclusion Act. Ironically, our Native Americans, the victims of the worst form of genocide, were perhaps the most difficult to enslave, because of long-cultivated independent survival skills in their rugged homeland. A brief history of the genocide of Native Americans is available at www.DisposableAmericans.com/NativeAmericans.

The most brutally enslaved people, African-Americans, face grave injustices yet today.

## Our Shameful Past

### 1859: A Slave Auction

In March, 1859 a slave auction[2] took place near Savannah, Georgia. Nearly five hundred slaves—men, women, children, and infants—were being auctioned off in an estate sale of two large plantations. The big event drew buyers from all over the south, and hotel rooms were quickly filled.

Horace Greeley, Editor of the *New York Tribune* and an abolitionist, reported on the proceedings: "The negroes were examined with as little consideration as if they had been brutes indeed; the buyers pulling their mouths open to see their teeth, pinching their limbs to find how muscular they were, walking them up and down to detect any signs of lameness, making them stoop and bend in different ways that they might be certain there was no concealed rupture or wound."

**FIGURE 6.1** Slave Auction in Atlanta, Georgia, 1864.
Photo by George N. Barnard (https://commons.wikimedia.org/wiki/File:Slave_Market-Atlanta_Georgia_1864.jpg).

The slaves were on their best behavior, hoping that they would attract a kind "mas'r." A man named Elisha did everything possible to keep his family together:

> Look at me, Mas'r; am prime rice planter; sho' you won't find a better man den me; no better on de whole plantation; not a bit old yet; do mo' work den ever; do carpenter work, too, little; better buy me, Mas'r; I'se be good sarvant, Mas'r. Molly, too, my wife, Sa, fus rate rice hand; mos as good as me. Stan' out yer, Molly, and let the gen'lm'n see...Show mas'r yer arm Molly—good arm dat mas'r—she do a heap of work mo' with dat arm yet. Let good mas'r see yer teeth Molly—see dat mas'r, teeth all reg'lar, all good—she'm young gal yet. Come out yer Israel, walk aroun' an' let the gen'lm'n see how spry you be.

Elisha then reached for his little three-year-old daughter, who was holding on to her mother's dress. *"Little Vardy's on'y a chile yet; make prime gal by-and-by. Better buy us mas'r, we'm fus' rate bargain."* But the kindly looking gentleman turned away from Elisha and his family.

The Negro slaves, all five hundred of them, stood nervously waiting as the buyers lit cigars and studied their log books, scanning the list of "chattel" available to them, preparing to start the bidding. The facial expression of each slave stepping on the auction block was the same—anguish about an unknown future, despair at the thought of never again seeing their loved ones.

The abject heartlessness of forever dividing families was captured by Mark Twain, when he sat on his front porch in 1874 and listened to his servant, Mary Ann Cord, whom the writer had come to know as "Aunt Rachel."

**FIGURE 6.2** Family of black American slaves in a field in Georgia, circa 1850.
New York Historical Society (https://commons.wikimedia.org/wiki/File:Family_of_slaves_in_
Georgia,_circa_1850.jpg).

Dey put chains on us an' put us on a stan' as high as dis po'ch,—twenty foot high,—an' all de people stood aroun', crowds an' crowds. An' dey'd come up dah an' look at us all roun', an' squeeze our arm, an' make us git up an' walk, an' den say, "Dis one too ole," or "Dis one lame," or "Dis one don't 'mount to much." An' dey sole my ole man, an' took him away, an' dey begin to sell my chil'en an' take dem away, an' I begin to cry; an' de man say, "Shet up yo' dam blubberin'," an' hit me on de mouf wid his han'. An' when de las' one was gone but my little Henry, I grab' him clost up to my breas' so, an' I ris up an' says, "You shan't take him away," I says; "I'll kill de man dat tetch him!" I says. But my little Henry whisper an' say, "I gwyne to run away, an' den I work an' buy yo' freedom." Oh, bless de chile, he always so good! But dey got him—dey got him, de men did; but I took and tear de clo'es mos' off of 'em, an' beat 'em over de head wid my chain; an' dey give it to me, too, but I didn't mine dat.

## 1908: Slavery by Another Name[3]

On March 30, 1908 twenty-two-year-old Green Cottenham was arrested in Alabama for "vagrancy." That means he couldn't prove, at the moment of his arrest, that he was employed. It was a tactic used by local sheriffs and judges to put black men in jail. Ironically, Green's arrest was on the anniversary of the 15th Amendment, which gave blacks the right to vote in 1870.

Cottenham was found guilty and sentenced to 30 days of hard labor. When he was unable to pay court and jailhouse fees, his sentence was extended to a full year, and he was sold to Tennessee Coal, a subsidiary of US Steel. The company forced him to live and work in a mineshaft deep in the black earth, where he worked every day from 3 a.m. to 8 p.m. digging and loading tons of coal. If he slowed down, he was whipped. He drank the water he was standing in. He was surrounded by pitch-dark caverns filled with poison gas and walls that often collapsed, crushing or suffocating miners. At night, he was chained to a wooden barracks. Crazed men were always nearby, filthy and sweaty, some homicidal, some sexual predators. A boy from the Alabama countryside had been cast into the center of hell.

## Lynchings[4]

**FIGURE 6.3** The burned body of 18-year-old Jesse Washington, Waco, Texas, May 15, 1916.
Library of Congress: Gildersleeve, Fred A., photographer (www.loc.gov/pictures/item/95517168/).

**FIGURE 6.4** A postcard of a Duluth lynching, June 15, 1920.
Photo courtesy of Minnesota Historical Society (http://news.minnesota.publicradio.org/projects/2001/06/lynching/page1.shtml).

**FIGURE 6.5** The charred corpse of Will Brown after being killed, mutilated and burned. September 28, 1919.
University of Washington (https://commons.wikimedia.org/wiki/File:Omaha_courthouse_lynching.jpg).

On May 25, 1911, the lynching of a black woman and her teenage son near Okemah, Oklahoma was photographed and printed on postcards as souvenirs. The victims were Laura and Lawrence Nelson. It is the only known surviving photograph of the lynching of a female.

A week earlier, Deputy Sheriff George Loney, a white man, had visited the Nelson farm to investigate a theft, and a fearful Lawrence shot the officer in the leg. Loney went untreated and bled to death. The two Nelsons were arrested and held in the Okemah jail. But in the early morning hours of May 25, a mob dragged them from their cells, raped Laura, and then hanged them over the side of a bridge. The mob reportedly included Charley Guthrie, the father of folk singer Woody Guthrie. The front page of that day's *Okemah Ledger* said the lynching was "executed with silent precision that makes it appear as a masterpiece of planning...The woman's arms were swinging by her side, untied, while about twenty feet away swung the boy with his clothes partly torn off and his hands tied with a saddle string...Gently swaying in the wind, the ghastly spectacle was discovered this morning by a negro boy taking his cow to water. Hundreds of people from Okemah and the western part of the county went to view the scene."

**FIGURE 6.6** The barefoot corpse of lynched Laura Nelson. May 25, 1911, Okemah, Oklahoma.

Photo postcard by G. H. Farnum (https://commons.wikimedia.org/wiki/File:Lynching_of_Laura_Nelson,_May_1911.jpg).

**FIGURE 6.7** The lynching of Laura and Lawrence Nelson, May 25, 1911, Okemah, Oklahoma.

Photo postcard by G. H. Farnum (https://commons.wikimedia.org/wiki/File:Lynching_of_Laura_Nelson_and_her_son_1.jpg).

**FIGURE 6.8** Lynching of Lawrence Nelson, May 25, 1911, Okemah, Oklahoma.
Photo postcard by G. H. Farnum (https://commons.wikimedia.org/wiki/File:Lawrence_Nelson_
high_res.jpg).

About 5,000 Americans were lynched between 1888 and 1968, the great majority black, about 150 of them women. A few lynching victims were young girls under the age of 15. Victims were often tortured with fire before being hanged, often for as little as asking for their rightful pay, for "throwing stones," or for "being a bad nigger." One pregnant African-American woman was hanged by the ankles and her unborn child ripped from her abdomen. Between the years 1880 and 1905, not a single person was convicted of a crime associated with these murders.

Lynchings were opposed by many whites, but rarely opposed in any meaningful way. For many others, the events were spectacles, even outings with umbrellas and picnic baskets. A postcard from the lynching of Jesse Washington in Waco, Texas in 1916 had a note on the back: "This is the Barbecue we had last night My picture is to the left with a cross over it your son Joe." On June 26, 1919, the Jackson, MS *Daily News* casually reported: "John Hatfield will be lynched by Ellisville mob at 5 o'clock this afternoon."

Blacks were largely powerless against the lynchings, except for a few courageous advocates for justice, such as Ida Wells, the editor of *Free Speech*. The *Memphis Daily Commercial Appeal* called her a "Black scoundrel," whites threatened to lynch the paper's owners, and a mob destroyed her printing press.

The *New Republic*[5] reported on the lynching of Jim Ivy, who had been charged with rape:

> Jim was staked with heavy chains and dry wood was piled knee-high around him. Gasoline tanks were tapped for fuel. Three men set the wood and Jim on fire. I saw the flames climb high on Jim. Jim screamed, prayed and cursed...I was looking into his eyes that second. They were popping with pain and terror...the flames reached up and burned his screaming voice into silence. The mob turned to go. It was about time for supper.

A white man stood proudly with the finger of a lynching victim in a jar. "We orter kill more of 'em around here," he blustered. "Teach 'em a lesson. Only way I see to stop raping is to keep on lynching. I'm goner put this finger on exhibition in my store window tomorrow, boys, and I want you to drop around...And don't forget to bring the ladies!"

Historian Leon Litwack said about the people doing the lynchings: "They were family men and women, good churchgoing folk who came to believe that keeping black people in their place was nothing less than pest control, a way of combating an epidemic or virus that if not checked would be detrimental to the health and security of the community."[6]

## The Present: Economic Lynching[7]

*The Washington Examiner* recently proclaimed, "Race relations in America have never been better."[8] In 2013, *The Economist* said, "Before the 1960s...most blacks were poor...almost none were to be found flourishing...None of that is true today."[9]

*The Wall Street Journal*, in its inimitable way, sputtered, "The civil-rights battles of the 1960s have been fought and won...The racial disparity that persists today...is evidence that too few blacks...have taken advantage of the opportunities now available to them."[10]

Many high-profile people in the media blame the most vulnerable among us for not helping themselves.

### Subjugation

Unfathomable wealth has been created since the recession—over $25 trillion[11]—a full third of the total wealth in our country today. The overwhelmingly white richest 10 percent took most of it.[12] Those Americans who oppose a wealth tax and a financial transaction tax continue to benefit from a stock market that offers almost nothing to hard-working, low-income minorities.

For every $100 owned by white households in 2013, black households had $8, a drop from $12 just three years earlier.[13] A 2014 study found that

African-American families had readily available liquid wealth of only $200, less than $1 for every $100 owned by whites.[14] Hispanic workers, who in 1979 made 81 cents for every dollar made by white workers, are now down to 69 cents. After the recession, they lost two-thirds of their household wealth because of plummeting home prices and foreclosures.[15]

We tend to believe that education is the great equalizer. But a middle-aged black person with a graduate degree has about the same odds of being a millionaire as a white person with only a high school diploma.[16]

The most vulnerable family members suffer the most. The infant mortality rate for African-Americans is more than double that for white children.[17] Almost half of black children under the age of six are living in poverty.[18] When black children in America finally get to school, they enter classrooms that are more segregated than in 1970, and poorly funded despite the Supreme Court mandate for public education to be "made available to all on equal terms." And, shockingly, over the past 20 years, the suicide rate for black children has nearly doubled, while decreasing significantly for white children.[19]

## Job Discrimination

The conservative solution for poverty is "get a job." But over half of the black college graduates of recent years were underemployed in 2013, working in occupations that typically do not require a four-year college degree.[20] Along with their sub-living-wage jobs, they have an average of almost $30,000 in student loan debt.

Too many black people can't find living-wage jobs, and a lot of it is due to racism. A recent study found that job applicants were about 50 percent more likely to be called back if they had "white" names.[21] A hiring analysis study found that white job applicants with criminal records were called back more often than blacks *without* criminal records.[22]

Among the 50 U.S. states, the highest unemployment rate for whites (West Virginia) was the same as the lowest unemployment rate for blacks (Virginia).[23]

## Modern Slavery

In "The New Jim Crow," Michelle Alexander documents the explosion of the prison population for drug offenses, with blacks and Hispanics the main targets, even though black and white crime rates for drugs, weapons, and assault are approximately the same, and perhaps even higher for whites. Yet blacks are arrested for drug offenses at three times the rate of whites.[24]

The 13th Amendment bans slavery "except as punishment for crime." The 14th Amendment bans debt servitude. But it doesn't matter to many of the profit makers. Inmates in modern-day private prisons generate tens of thousands of dollars a year in revenue, and private prisons sell inmate labor for as little as

17 cents an hour to corporations like Chevron, Bank of America, AT&T, and IBM.[25] Nearly a million prisoners work in factories and call centers. More corporate profits come from the probation business, which, in direct opposition to the 14th Amendment, keeps people in prison for being too poor to pay their court costs and probation fees. It's called debt slavery. It's a modern and more "civilized" form of the long American tradition of shortening the lives of poor minorities, especially black people.[26]

## Long-Term Lynching

Many studies have documented the link between financial stress and illness, and between economic status and longevity.[27]

The sickening—or deadly—effect of poverty among minorities is manifested in numerous ways.[28] Low-income people of color breathe dirtier air; they are less likely to have health insurance; they are three times more likely to be victimized by crime; they suffer stress loads that make it much more difficult to work themselves out of poverty; in Detroit, where payments to Wall Street were approaching a half-billion dollars, thousands of black residents couldn't even get water.

## Race: Personal

Reminiscing[29] on a Christmas-time gathering of +60-year-old business school grads in 2010:

> We grew up as white educated males in the most productive country in the world in the most prosperous time of history. We were idealistic, angry at the leaders who took us to Vietnam, distrusting anyone over 30, vowing to change the world. Even those of us who were irresponsible party-loving laggards in college had jobs waiting for us when we left school (with or without a degree). We couldn't fail even if we wanted to.
>
> And change the world we did. The business people of our generation were the greatest part of the Reagan-era "government is the problem" attitude that deregulated the financial industry and allowed our savvy white educated minds to shape the future of investment gains and tax avoidance. We bought into Ayn Rand's "greed is good" philosophy. We felt justified when Milton Friedman and Arthur Laffer told us, against all common sense, that decreasing taxes on the wealthy would generate revenues that would trickle down to the rest of America.
>
> Our successes became well-deserved in our minds, our accomplishments a tribute to our own initiative and hard work. After all, we had made it. Let today's young people be more like us.

In his book, *White Like Me*, author Tim Wise described the privileged family history of a white educated American male.[30]

> When I graduated from college...I was hired as a Youth Coordinator for the Louisiana Coalition Against Racism and Nazism.
>
> I knew the two guys who started the organization...Had I not known Larry and Lance, there is no way I could have gotten that job, in which case I could never have built up a reputation for doing antiracism work... and I surely wouldn't have been asked to do this book.
>
> Well, I knew them, of course, because I had gone to school at Tulane; but how had I gotten there? After all, my family was far from wealthy, and even then Tulane was extremely expensive.
>
> It helps...when one's mother is able to go down to the bank and take out a loan for $10,000.
>
> But how does one's mother get such a loan?
>
> Well it helps...if one's mother's mother can co-sign for the loan...my grandmother, who was able to use her house as collateral against the loan.
>
> But how did my grandmother get that house, having never worked outside the home during her adult life? Well, to her great fortune, she had been married to a man who did: my grandfather, who had been career military and then a Corps of Engineers employee.
>
> So in a very real sense, my grandmother's house—without which I would not have gone to Tulane, met Larry and Lance, gotten the job... built up a reputation as an antiracist, and gotten out on lecture circuit—was there to be used as because we were white.
>
> Although not every white person's story is the same as mine, the simple truth is that any white person born before 1964, at least, was legally elevated above any person of color, and as such received directly the privileges, the head start, the advantages of whiteness as a matter of course. This goes for all whites, not merely some, but all. Even the white poor received the benefit of at least being considered superior to black people...

## Notes

1   "New Perspectives on the West." Public Broadcasting System.
2   "Slave Auction, 1859." EyeWitnessToHistory.com, from *New York Daily Tribune*, March 9, 1859 reprinted in Hart, Albert B., *American History Told by Contemporaries*, 1928; Mark Twain, "A True Story, Repeated Word for Word as I Heard It." Public Broadcasting System.
3   "The Untold History of Post-Civil War 'Neoslavery!'" National Public Radio, March 25, 2008; Blackmon, Douglas A., *Slavery by Another Name: The Re-Enslavement of Black Americans from the Civil War to World War II* Reprint Edition. Anchor, 2009.
4   Weiser, Kathy, *Lynchings & Hangings of America*. Legends of America, updated 2015.

5 "Lynching of Jim Ivy." *The New Republic*, July 22, 1931.

6 Litwack, Leon, "Hell Hounds." In Allen, James (Editor), *Without Sanctuary: Lynching Photography in America*. Twin Palms Press, 2000.

7 Buchheit, Paul, "Two Other Ways Racists Kill." Commondreams.org, June 22, 2015; Buchheit, Paul, "Economic Lynching." NationofChange.org, July 14, 2014.

8 Hannan, Dan, "Race Relations in America Have Never Been Better." *Washington Examiner*, April 13, 2015.

9 "Unequal Protection." *The Economist*, April 27, 2013.

10 Riley, Jason L., "Drawing the Wrong Lessons from Selma about America Today." *Wall Street Journal*, March 10, 2015.

11 Credit Suisse. *Global Wealth Databook*, 2013, 2014, 2015.

12 "Working for the Few," Oxfam, January 20, 2014.

13 Kochhar, Rakesh and Fry, Richard, "Wealth Inequality has Widened along Racial, Ethnic Lines Since End of Great Recession." Pew Research, December 12, 2014.

14 "Beyond Broke," Duke Center for Global Policy Solutions, April 2014.

15 "Underwater America," Haas Institute, 2014.

16 Stilwell, Victoria, "What Are Your Odds of Becoming a Millionaire?" Bloomberg Business, January 21, 2016.

17 "Infant, Neonatal, and Postneonatal Mortality Rates." Centers for Disease Control, 2013.

18 Mishel, Lawrence; Bivens, Josh; Gould, Elise; and Shierholz, Heidi, *The State of Working America, 12th Edition*. A forthcoming Economic Policy Institute book. Cornell University Press.

19 Bridge, Jeffrey A.; Asti, Lindsey; Horowitz, Lisa; Greenhouse, Joel B.; Fontanella, Cynthia A.; Sheftall, Arielle H.; Kelleher, Kelly J.; Campo, John Vincent, "Suicide Trends Among Elementary School-Aged Children in the United States from 1993 to 2012." JAMA Network, July 2015.

20 Jones, Janelle and Schmitt, John, "A College Degree is No Guarantee." Center for Economic and Policy Research, May 2014.

21 Mullainathan, Sendhil, "Racial Bias, Even When We Have Good Intentions." *New York Times*, January 3, 2015.

22 Pager, Devah, "The Mark of a Criminal Record." *American Journal of Sociology*, Vol. 108, No. 5 (March 2003), pp. 937–975.

23 Wilson, Valerie, "State Unemployment Rates by Race and Ethnicity at the End of 2015 Show a Plodding Recovery." *Economic Policy Institute*, February 11, 2016.

24 Alexander, Michelle, *The New Jim Crow: Mass Incarceration in the Age of Colorblindness*. The New Press, 2012.

25 Pelaez, Vicky, "The Prison Industry in the United States: Big Business or a New Form of Slavery?" *Global Research*, March 31, 2014.

26 "In for a Penny: The Rise of America's New Debtors' Prisons." *American Civil Liberties Union*, October 2010.

27 "Financial Wellness and Health Care Costs," *Financial Finesse*, March 2011; Johan P. Mackenbach, "Only the Poor Die Young." Project Syndicate, June 17, 2013; "The Growing Gap in Life Expectancy by Income." *National Academies of Sciences, Engineering, and Medicine*, 2015; Bosworth, Barry, Burtless, Gary, and Zhang, Kan, "The Growing Gap in Longevity between Rich and Poor and Its Impact on

Redistribution through Social Security." The Brookings Institution, 2016; Chetty, Raj; Stepner, Michael; Abraham, Sarah; Lin, Shelby; Scuderi, Benjamin; Turner, Nicholas; Bergeron, Augustin; Cutler, David, "The Association Between Income and Life Expectancy in the United States, 2001–2014." *Journal of the American Medical Association*, April 10, 2016.

28  Buchheit, Paul, "Economic Lynching." Op. cit.

29  Author's personal anecdote.

30  Wise, Tim. *White Like Me: Reflections on Race from a Privileged Son*. Soft Skull Press, 2011.

## Bibliography

Alexander, Michelle, *The New Jim Crow: Mass Incarceration in the Age of Colorblindness*. The New Press, 2012.

Benforado, Adam, *Unfair: The New Science of Criminal Injustice*. Crown, 2015.

Blackmon, Douglas A., *Slavery by Another Name: The Re-Enslavement of Black Americans from the Civil War to World War II* Reprint Edition. Anchor, 2009.

Glaude Jr., Eddie S., *Democracy in Black: How Race Still Enslaves the American Soul*. Crown, 2016.

Jackson, Thomas F., *From Civil Rights to Human Rights: Martin Luther King, Jr., and the Struggle for Economic Justice*. University of Pennsylvania Press, 2007.

Lewis, Pamela, *Teaching While Black*. Empire State Editions, 2016.

Nair, Yasmin, *The Postracial Delusion*. Monthly Review Press, 2016.

Shapiro, Thomas M., *The Hidden Cost of Being African American: How Wealth Perpetuates Inequality*. Oxford University Press, 2004.

Wise, Tim. *White Like Me: Reflections on Race from a Privileged Son*. Soft Skull Press, 2011.

# 7

# RACISM AND NARCISSISM[1]

While Edward Snowden, Chelsea Manning and John Kiriakou are vilified for revealing vital information about spying, bombing, and torture, a man who conspired with Goldman Sachs to make billions of dollars on the planned failure of subprime mortgages[2] was honored by New York University for his "Outstanding Contributions to Society."[3]

## 1. Narcissism

Studies have consistently shown that increased wealth causes people to turn inward, to believe more in their own "superior" traits, and to care less about the feelings and needs of others.[4] This anti-social attitude blends well with the Ayn-Randish "greed is good" message of unregulated capitalism.

Experiments by Paul Piff and his colleagues have revealed that upper-class individuals tend to be narcissistic, with a clear sense of entitlement.[5] Worse yet, they believe their talents and attributes—*genius*, even—have earned them a rightful position of status over everyone else.[6]

Scarier yet, according to one study, the American sense of entitlement has been *growing* over the past 30 years, despite the fact that most of us have lost ground to the super-rich.[7] And *most* disturbing is that "upper-class" individuals tend to behave more unethically than average citizens.[8]

Other studies have determined that money pushes people further to the right, making them less egalitarian, less willing to provide broad educational opportunities to all members of society, and a big part of the reason that our investment in public infrastructure as a component of GDP dropped by 60 percent from 1968 to 2011.[9]

As the super-rich take their helicopters to and from work, they're having multi-million-dollar bunkers built under their houses to protect them from the masses.[10]

## 2. Delusion

The mainstream media's unwillingness to state the truth about inequality has led people to vastly underestimate the wealth gap in our country, guessing that the poorest 40 percent own about 10 percent of the wealth, when in reality they own much less than one percent of the wealth. Out of every dollar, they own a third of a penny.[11]

Free-marketers overwhelm us with their delusions:[12]

Income inequality is simply not a significant problem.

(*The Wall Street Journal*)

Income inequality in a capitalist system is truly beautiful...

(*The Washington Post*'s George Will, quoting John Tamny)

Capitalism has worked very well.

(Bill Gates)

A free market system...ensures a fair, democratic process.

(Sarah Palin)

Let the market do its job.

(*Chicago Tribune*)

Many wealthy Americans believe that the state of the country is reflected in the stock market. But the richest 10 percent own over 90 percent of the stocks and mutual funds.[13] No problem for the Koch Foundation, which "comforts" us with the knowledge that an American earning over $34,000 a year is part of the wealthiest one percent in the world.[14]

## 3. Condescension

Members of the sinking middle class in our pathologically unequal society may well find it convenient to blame people in lower economic classes, who are unlikely to fight back. Guidance for such condescension comes, as noted earlier, from Charles Murray, who ignores the family stress caused by the lack of educational and employment opportunities, and instead accuses the poor of having a "genetic makeup that is significantly different from the configuration of the population above the poverty line."[15] And, he adds, "Married, educated people who work hard and conscientiously raise their kids shouldn't hesitate to voice their disapproval of those who defy these norms."

This appeals to people like Paul Ryan and Scott Walker, both of whom compared the safety net to a "hammock," and John Boehner, who explained the thinking of poor people: "I really don't have to work...I think I'd rather just sit around."[16]

The critics of struggling Americans should be reminded that the cost of the entire safety net is only about ONE-SIXTH of the $2.2 trillion in tax avoidance that primarily benefits the rich.[17]

A good American capitalist like Republican Senator Lindsey Graham would say, "It's really American to avoid paying taxes, legally...It's a game we play."

It's a game for the people looking down on a troubled nation.

### 4. Extreme Racism[18]

As more and more immigrants entered the country in the early twentieth century, supposedly learned Americans, convinced of their superior genes, began to decry the "dilution" of advanced races due to gradual inbreeding. To ward off the imminent decline of society, procreation would have to be carefully controlled. Sterilization and mass incarceration were proposed, along with immigration reform. This was the height of the eugenics movement.

Some unlikely figures swelled the ranks of the eugenicists, including Margaret Sanger, W.E.B. DuBois, George Bernard Shaw, several prominent scientists and physicians, and a majority of the 1927 Supreme Court. Teddy Roosevelt said, "Society has no business to permit degenerates to reproduce their kind." Herbert Hoover added, "One white man equals from two to three of the colored races." By 1927, Ellis Island was turning away more people than it was admitting.

While attitudes toward minority groups may not have changed much over the years, the inflammatory language has been muted, and the excessively brutal treatment of targeted "inferiors" has largely ended. Although perhaps not. Young black men were nine times more likely than other groups of Americans to be killed by police officers in 2015.[19] Millions of Americans cheered on Donald Trump when he dismissed Mexican immigrants as rapists.[20] Incarceration of minorities has reached its peak in just the last 20 years, and the passion for immigration reform continues to grow with irrational fears of Muslim terrorism. Ominously, sterilization laws still exist in 20 states.

### Notes

1   Buchheit, Paul, "Why So Many Americans Defend the Failed Capitalist Experiment." Truthout Buzzflash, September 14, 2015.

2   McQuaig, Linda and Brooks, Neil, *Billionaires' Ball: Gluttony and Hubris in an Age of Epic Inequality*. Beacon Press, 2012.

3 Martens, Pam, "Wall Street Is Corrupting Everything—Even University Commencements." *Wall Street on Parade*, May 15, 2015.

4 "Social Class as Culture." Association for Psychological Science, August 8, 2011; Grewal, Daisy, "How Wealth Reduces Compassion." *Scientific American*, April 10, 2012.

5 Piff, Paul K., "Wealth and the Inflated Self: Class, Entitlement, and Narcissism." *Personality and Social Psychology Bulletin*, December 19, 2013.

6 Holland, Joshua, "Why the Wealthy Favor Harsh Punishment—for Criminals and Errant Schoolchildren. Bill Moyers & Co., January 13, 2014.

7 Gray, Peter, "Why is Narcissism Increasing among Young Americans?" *Psychology Today*, January 16, 2014.

8 Piff, Paul K.; Stancatoa, Daniel M.; Côtéb, Stéphane; Mendoza-Dentona, Rodolfo; Keltner, Dacher, "Higher Social Class Predicts Increased Unethical Behavior." University of California, January 26, 2012.

9 Page, Benjamin I., Bartels, Larry M., and Seawright, Jason, "Democracy and the Policy Preferences of Wealthy Americans." Northwestern University, March 2013; Oswald, Andrew J. and Powdthavee, Nattavudh, "Money Makes People Right-Wing and Inegalitarian." *VoxEU*, February 13, 2014; Madland, David and Bunker, Nick, "Ties that Bind: How a Strong Middle Class Supports Strong Public Infrastructure." Center for American Progress, March 22, 2012.

10 Brennan, Morgan, "Billionaire Bunkers: Security for the Super-Rich." Forbes, December 6, 2013.

11 Norton, Michael I. and Ariely, Dan, "Building a Better America—One Wealth Quintile at a Time." *Perspectives on Psychological Science*, 2011.

12 Buchheit, Paul, "Why So Many Americans Defend..." Op. cit.

13 Wolff, Edward N., "Household Wealth Trends in the United States, 1962–2013: What Happened over the Great Recession?" National Bureau of Economic Research, December 2014.

14 Winograd, David, "Charles Koch Foundation: An Income of $34,000 Puts You in The Wealthiest 1 Percent." *Huffington Post*, July 11, 2013.

15 "Charles Murray." Southern Poverty Law Center.

16 Delaney, Arthur and McAuliff, Michael, "Paul Ryan Wants 'Welfare Reform Round 2.'" *Huffington Post*, March 20, 2012; "Scott Walker: Safety Net Has Become 'A Hammock.'" Bloomberg, February 23, 2015; Krugman, Paul, "A Conservative Disdain for the Unemployed." Truthout.org, September 27, 2014.

17 "Policy Basics: Where Do Our Federal Tax Dollars Go?" Center on Budget and Policy Priorities, March 4, 2016.

18 Black, Edwin, "War Against the Weak: Eugenics and America's Campaign to Create a Master Race." *Dialog Press*, 2012; Maxwell, Anne, "Picture Imperfect: Photography and Eugenics, 1879–1940." *Sussex Academic Press*, 2010; Bryson, Bill, "One Summer: America 1927." *Anchor Books*, 2013; "Eugenics." Wikipedia.com, accessed 2016.

19 Swaine, Jon; Laughland, Oliver; Lartey, Jamiles; and McCarthy, Ciara: "Young Black Men Killed by US Police at Highest Rate in Year of 1,134 Deaths." *The Guardian*, December 31, 2015.

20 Ye Hee Lee, Michelle, "Donald Trump's False Comments Connecting Mexican Immigrants and Crime." *Washington Post*, July 8, 2015.

# 8

# THE SICK AND THE ELDERLY

## The Past: Flu[1] and Polio[2]

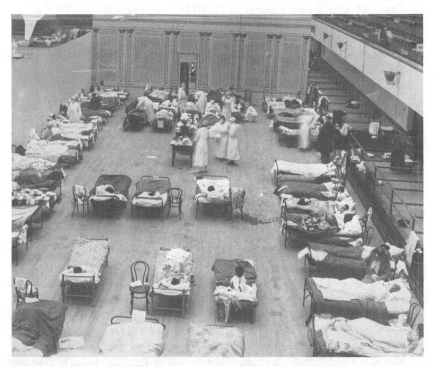

**FIGURE 8.1** 1918 flu epidemic: the Oakland Municipal Auditorium in use as a temporary hospital.
Photo by Edward A. "Doc" Rogers. Joseph R. Knowland collection, Oakland Public Library (https://commons.wikimedia.org/wiki/File:1918_flu_in_Oakland.jpg).

About a century ago, on March 4, 1918, a U.S. army cook by the name of Albert Gitchell was admitted to a military hospital at Fort Riley, Kansas. Doctors had no idea that they were treating the first known case of Spanish flu, which would devastate the population of the world, killing up to fifty million people, or about three percent of the human race.

A week after Gitchell entered the hospital, about five hundred more soldiers with the same symptoms were being treated. All around the U.S., cases began appearing—mostly members of the military, returning from the war. That spring, 48 soldiers, all healthy in February, died at Fort Riley. Some believe it was caused by the soldiers burning tons of manure and releasing the virus through the air. Some believe the Germans had planted the germ of influenza. Whatever the cause, the flu spread quickly throughout Europe, too, but most countries were reluctant to frighten their citizens with the announcement of a fast-spreading sickness. Only Spain reported it, and as a result people around the world got the false impression that Spain was the source of the problem.

The medical community wasn't prepared for the outbreak. Fears grew rapidly in the U.S. as government officials, uncertain of causes and potential effects, advised the public to wear masks, and for schools and churches and theaters, and even stores, to limit the number of patrons. But people were coming to the doctor's office for treatment and dying twelve hours later. Doctors had waiting rooms full of patients they didn't know how to treat. So people began to fashion their own medicines out of kerosene, vinegar, honey—anything that gave a family the slightest tinge of hope. But nothing worked. Meanwhile, the flu was attacking entire households, workplaces, church groups, army stations. Dr. Shirley Fannin, an epidemiologist, explained, "If an individual with influenza were standing in front of a room full of people coughing, each cough would carry millions of particles with disease-causing organisms into the air...It doesn't take very long for one case to become 10,000 cases."

It got to the point that people refused to talk to each other for fear of breathing in the disease.

A nurse at Great Lakes Naval Station near Chicago saw soldiers lying on the floor waiting for the boys in the beds to die. They were delirious with fever, short of breath, bleeding profusely through their noses.

Children who survived lived on with vivid memories. Anna Milani recalled: "It was a mild day and we were sitting on the step. [Across from us a] 15-year-old girl was just buried. Towards the evening, we heard a lot of screaming going on and in that same house a little baby, 18 months old, passed away in that same family." Another child, William Maxwell, recounted: "I would wake up and it would be daylight and I'd wake up, the next time I woke up it would be dark and it might be dark when I woke up, it might be daylight, I had no sense of day and night." Children recited a little rhyme: "I had a little bird, its name was Enza, I opened up the window, and in flew Enza."

William Sardo remembered that many of his neighbors didn't make it: "These were friends of yours that were passing away, these were whole families that you knew, these were people that you went to school with or church with. It was very eerie, very, very eerie." Eerier still in Philadelphia, where death carts appeared on the streets, like a scene from the Black Plague. Many of the dead lay for a time in the gutter.

Medical labs worked feverishly to find a bacterial vaccine, but the Spanish flu was caused by a virus, and little was known about viruses in 1918. Normally, strains of flu most severely impact the very young and very old. This flu was different. It was caused, researchers eventually determined, by an overreaction of the immune system—the stronger the immune system, the greater the reaction. The first victims were vigorous young men who had lived together and fought together for many months in the trenches of Europe. Compounding the problem was that many of them were malnourished. Their immune systems were under great stress from the virus and from their already weakened conditions.

Much of the world was beginning to shut down, as fear of infection kept people inside their houses for weeks, stepping outside only for the barest necessities, and then with masks in place, and while keeping respectable distances from others. Every person's nightmare was to wake up with the flu and die by nightfall. So many died that communities around the U.S. were short of caskets. Some undertakers hired guards to stay with the coffins. Preachers declared Armageddon, the end of the world, and even the U.S. Surgeon General agreed that civilization was in danger of being wiped out. Today, the media would likely be filled with cries of terrorism.

Then it just disappeared, as quickly as it came, even though no cure had been found. It was believed that the virus was mutating so quickly that it suddenly became dominated by a less lethal form. By now it was also known that most deaths came not from the virus itself, but from an accompanying case of pneumonia, which began to be treated vigorously.

Whatever the cause, it had been the deadliest flu ever, infecting up to a half-billion people, more than a quarter of the world, and killing up to fifty million human beings. Some locations, such as Western Samoa, had infection rates of 90 percent or more. The overall impact rivals the Black Death of the Middle Ages. In a sense, it was worse, for it spread throughout the world, and more people died than in the previous four years of war; ironically, the potency of the flu in Germany and Austria may have hastened their retreat from the military conflict. Together, the war and the Spanish flu had disrupted agriculture and manufacturing around the world. The overwhelming sense of relief that spread through the world at the end of the epidemic was comparable to that of the war's end.

## Polio

*Safe, effective, and potent.* That was the verdict of the Polio Vaccine Evaluation Center on April 12, 1955.[3] The threat of paralysis or even death from polio would be almost totally eliminated in a few short years.

**FIGURE 8.2** Physical therapist is assisting two polio-stricken children.
Centers for Disease Control and Prevention's Public Health Image Library (https://commons.
wikimedia.org/wiki/File:Polio_physical_therapy.jpg).

The American people had lived in fear of this dreaded disease, especially since President Franklin Roosevelt had contracted it in the 1920s. Some responses defied common sense: people sprayed the pesticide DDT and walked around with bandanas on their faces. But those who were suddenly stricken had reason to panic.

The two leading researchers at the time were Jonas Salk and Albert Sabin. Sabin was openly hostile toward his competitor, going so far as to criticize and demean Salk at a conference presentation. When the March of Dimes decided to field test Salk's vaccine, the stunned Sabin objected, claiming, "This vaccine isn't ready to be tested. We should wait five more years. We should wait 10 more years." But two million children were successfully inoculated. After the April 12, 1955 announcement, parents and teachers cheered, factory whistles blew, and Jonas Salk was considered an American hero, a superstar of sorts, frequently cheered by passengers on airlines, and usually upgraded to hotel penthouses.

Yet Sabin had his chance to say "I told you so," at least for a little while. Within a month of the evaluation center announcement, thousands of children became sick. Hundreds were paralyzed. Some even died. Use of Salk's vaccine was immediately suspended. But it turned out that a California company, Cutter Labs, eager to get its product on the market, had produced a batch with a virulent, LIVE virus. Cutter was not solely to blame; shoddy government screening had allowed the deadly batch to pass inspection.

Application of the Salk vaccine resumed, and went on to preserve the health and save the lives of millions of people.

## The Present: The Middle Class Getting Sicker[4]

From 1978 to 1998, mortality rates were falling throughout the entire developed world, thanks in good part to advances in health care. Then began a disturbing trend[5] for U.S. middle-aged whites, primarily the less-educated, many of whom made up the solid middle class of years before. Their mortality rate went up. A 50-year-old lower-income man can expect to live a full 13 years less than a man in the upper-income class.[6] This hasn't happened in other countries, and it didn't happen to blacks or Hispanics in the U.S. (although the mortality rate for blacks is still much higher than for whites). And the reasons aren't clear. But the link to economic stress is almost certain.

### The Terror of Inadequate Health Care

The FBI defines terrorism as "Acts dangerous to human life...intended to intimidate or coerce a civilian population."[7] Much of the behavior of our current health care system meets that definition. The facts show intention on the part of corporations to charge whatever they like for their medical products and services, and to coerce the public into accepting the current system as the only option.

### The Cost of Private Health Care is about Half of Household Income

According to the Milliman Medical Index, the cost of health care in 2015 for a typical American family of four covered by a PPO was $24,671—*nearly half the median household income*. Over $10,000 of this was paid directly by the family, through payroll deductions and time-of-service expenses.[8]

### In Addition to $10K Out-of-Pocket, a Typical Family Pays $4,000 for Medical Fraud and Subsidies

Medical billing fraud is estimated at ten percent of all health care, or about $270 billion, while patent monopolies raise the price of prescription drugs by another $270 billion a year.[9] Combined, this represents an astonishing annual cost of over $4,000 to an average American household. As *The Atlantic* puts it, "The people most likely to bilk the system are doctors and medical providers, not 'welfare queens.'"[10]

## Most Elderly Americans Can't Afford Life-Saving Drugs

An AARP study of 115 specialty drugs found that the average cost of a year's worth of prescriptions was over $50,000, three times more than the average Social Security benefit.[11] Although it's true that most people don't pay the full retail cost of medicine, the portion paid by insurance companies is ultimately passed on to consumers through higher premiums.

## One in Four Americans Suffer Mental Illness; Mental Health Facilities Cut by 90 Percent

According to the National Alliance on Mental Illness,[12] 25 percent of adults experience mental illness in a given year, with almost half of the homeless population so affected. Yet from 1970 to 2002, the per capita number of public mental health hospital beds plummeted from over 200 per 100,000 to 20 per 100,000, and after the recession, state cutbacks continued.[13]

For the increasing number of Americans with **mental health problems**, there is no one to turn to.[14] The Department of Health and Human Services reports that most U.S. counties "have no practicing psychiatrists, psychologists, or social workers."[15] In 44 of the 50 states, the majority of mentally ill people **reside in jails rather than in psychiatric hospitals**.[16]

## Intimidation by Outrageous Markups

In a recent analysis of 50 hospitals (49 for-profit) with the highest charge-to-cost ratios in 2012, the average markup was 1,000 percent, which means that a procedure costing a hospital $100 is marked up to $1,000 for us.[17]

Some of the markups test the limits of sanity: an 80-cent needle goes for $143.25 (a 17,000 percent markup), a 25-cent IUD device for $1,000, a $10 blood test for $10,000 at another hospital. After Gilead Sciences was criticized for charging $1,000 for a hepatitis pill that costs $10 in Egypt, the company responded by introducing a new pill that costs $1,350. When pharmaceutical CEO Martin Shkreli raised the price of an anti-infection AIDS drug from $13.50 to $750 a tablet, a competitor announced the availability of a substitute drug for $1 per tablet.[18]

A Johns Hopkins professor explained, "They are marking up the prices because no one is telling them they can't."[19]

## Deception and Coercion

Pharmaceutical companies have successfully lobbied Congress to keep Medicare from bargaining for lower drug prices.[20] Americans are further exploited when corporations pay off generic drug manufacturers to delay entry of their products into the market, thereby forcing consumers to pay the highest prices for medicine.

We're deceived again by certificate-of-need laws, which force many patients to accept established money-making procedures while denying access to modern technologies such as virtual colonoscopies.[21]

And cheated yet again when the doctors we trust accept payoffs from pharmaceutical companies to promote the most expensive products.

## The Terror of Poverty Without Health Care

Uninsurance can be deadly.[22] Low-income minorities are least likely to have coverage, and the resulting financial stress, as documented by over two hundred studies,[23] leads to sickness and early death. Over 40 percent of uninsured adults of color would be eligible for Medicaid if the program were adopted by all states.[24]

But it's not just the uninsured who feel the terror of unattainable health care. About half of privately insured Americans report experiencing financial hardship as a result of health care costs,[25] and nearly half (43 percent) of sick Americans skipped doctor's visits and/or medication purchases in 2012 because of excessive costs.[26] Many Americans can't afford essential care. About half (40 to 60 percent) of Americans *don't have savings available* to cover a visit to the emergency room.[27] Many Americans are turning to alcohol, which is killing people at a rate not seen in 35 years.[28]

As a further testament to the ills of privatizing patient care, some emergency services are now being run, often with disastrous results, by private equity firms, whose primary concern is to turn a profit while "caring" for people in their most vulnerable moments.[29]

## The Best Medical Care in the World—for the Wealthy

According to Dr. Samuel Dickman, lead author of a comprehensive study on health care inequality:

> We spend more on medical care than in any other country, and those dollars are increasingly concentrated on the wealthy...[we are] forcing poor and middle-class Americans to choose between paying rent, buying groceries, or going to the doctor...[30]

Wealth promotes health. Super wealth buys an emergency room for the mansion or yacht or private plane, equipped with scanners, ultrasounds, x-ray machines, and blood analyzers. Or, if a hospital stay is needed, one fine option is a $2,400 suite with a butler in the hospital's penthouse.[31]

Not all of "concierge medicine" is so extravagant. Basic signup fees range from $1,500 to $25,000 per year, with premium memberships offering unrestricted online access to a doctor, although with extra charges for face-to-face services. It's still out of the question for almost all of us.

Yet, in a farcical display of trickle-down wishfulness, Forbes proclaims that "these elite concierge medical practices are trailblazing methodologies and technologies that will, in time, be available to everyone."[32] Little chance with a privatized system.

## Discarding the Elderly

Elder abuse is defined as "harmful acts toward an elderly adult, such as physical abuse, sexual abuse, emotional or psychological abuse, financial exploitation, and neglect." Financial exploitation comes from the banking industry; neglect emanates from the halls of Congress.

### "The Greatest Retirement Crisis in the History of the World"[33]

That's what Forbes calls it.[34] Over half of households age 55 and older have no 401(k) or IRA or other retirement savings.[35]

Since 2009, $30 trillion in new wealth has been gained in the U.S., six times more than the amount spent on Social Security during that time, and most of it went to older Americans, as it has for the last 30 years. But most of it went to a relatively few people who were already rich. According to the Economic Policy Institute, "the median retirement savings...for all households is close to zero since nearly half of households have no savings in these accounts." Even the upper-middle class (second-highest quartile) is in trouble, with a median retirement fund, by one estimate, of only $6,000. The National Institute on Retirement Security puts the median retirement account at $12,000 for near-retirement households.[36]

And it's getting worse. The percentage of 75- to 84-year-old seniors falling into poverty doubled from 2005 to 2009. That was *before* the recession. A recent Rutgers study found that "inequality is higher after age 64, and is especially apparent after age 74."[37]

## Adding to the Insanity: The Threat of Social Security Cuts

Income, for most elderly Americans, comes largely from Social Security. Almost three-quarters of single Social Security recipients 65 or older depend on Social Security for all or most of their income,[38] which averages only about $1,300 per month. Global AgeWatch reports that income security for U.S. seniors is among the worst in the developed world.[39]

It has been estimated that without Social Security benefits, 45 percent of seniors would have incomes below the poverty line.[40] Yet the popular and effective program is always under fire by Congress and business for being a wasteful "entitlement." In reality, it's an earned benefit, paid for by lifetime workers who often pay more than they get back, and ultimately providing the major source of income for most of the elderly.[41]

The number of Americans who expect Social Security to be a primary source of retirement income has increased by 40 percent over the past ten years (25 percent to 35 percent).[42] The program needs bolstering, not cutting. This could be accomplished through the *removal of the payroll tax ceiling*.

## Our Elderly Victims: Too Poor to See a Doctor

Poverty can be fatal. It's estimated that nearly 45,000 Americans die every year because they can't afford health insurance.[43] Numerous recent academic and government studies have found a clear link between inequality and longevity, up to a *15-year difference in life expectancy between the richest and poorest males*.[44] Compared to other developed countries, we're continually losing ground, as our ranking has dropped on nearly every major health measure.[45]

In today's America, even being middle class can be detrimental to one's health and longevity. Beginning in 1998, as noted earlier, the death rates of middle-aged white non-Hispanic Americans began to rise, especially among the less-educated. That didn't happen in other countries.

Walmart cashier Michelle Croy remembers watching seniors having to decide between buying food and buying medicine.[46] An agonizing choice: stay hungry or stay sick.

## Personal Stories[47]

Wealth abounds among the seniors in Naples, Florida, but so does poverty, according to a PBS *News Hour* report. Financial problems for the elderly often stem from medical issues that aren't covered by insurance.

Former jeweler Harry Knight and his wife Sarah, both in their mid-70s, came to Naples after selling their home in New Jersey. All went well for a while, as their modest income was supplemented by Harry's job at a local grocery store. But failing health turned their lives around. She had Crohn's disease and temporal arteritis (inflamed arteries), and he was diagnosed with early-onset Alzheimer's disease; also, he lost his job after an argument with his manager.

The Knights get $17 per month from the recently cut food stamp program. They were forced to turn to a charity group, the Jewish Family and Community Services (JFCS) of southwest Florida, for food and basic senior services. But they're falling behind by $700 per month, largely because of the cost of their medicines. "All my life, I've struggled," Sarah said. "So now, in my 70s, I have to struggle all over again? It bothered me a lot. In fact, I felt suicidal—that's why I'm going to a therapist."

Harry and Sarah are not alone. Angelo and Mina Maffucci, both around eighty years of age, lost much of their savings in the mortgage collapse, and, like the Knights, they have unmanageable medical bills for Angelo's back injury and prostate cancer. Forced to live in an apartment owned by their son, they face financial problems for the first time at an age when only charity can provide their needs. "We hated to ask, you know? We didn't know where to go, because we didn't...ever have a problem like this before," Mina said. They live now on Social Security, food stamps, occasional help from their son, and assistance from the JFCS senior center.

Dorothy Abruzzo, a widow for over twenty years, was prosperous at one time, paying cash for a condo and helping her financially strapped daughter, and holding down a good job at a luxury dress shop. But emergency carotid artery surgery and a mismanaged retirement fund left her in the same position as the Knights and the Maffuccis, dependent on food stamps. She spoke sadly, "I never in my life thought I would have needed charity...83 and I'm renting and on food stamps...I've put myself on a [food] budget—$159 for the whole month."

A 94-year-old woman who wished to stay anonymous told her story: an efficiency apartment, $70 per month in food stamps, and, of course, assistance from JFCS. She needs a constant supply of oxygen in order to breathe. "I do everything alone. I go shopping alone, still drive a car. I'm very independent. That's the thing that bothers me. At one time, I was in control. But the recession has done terrible things."

Jaclynn Faffer, CEO of JFCS, which has 676 members, estimated that about 60 percent of them are at or below the poverty line. "Seniors are living longer, and they're outliving their incomes," she said. "And, unlike younger people, who we can help find a job, find more affordable housing, with our seniors, that just can't happen."

Lisa Salo, a kindergarten teacher in Suwanee, Georgia, was diagnosed with breast cancer. She didn't have enough insurance to pay for it. With bills of over $4,000 a month coming in, and with Lisa and her husband making just enough to support two kids and pay the mortgage, the collection agencies started calling. A sympathetic parent at Lisa's school set up a website "crowdfunding" page, which raised almost $7,000. But cancer treatment costs an average of over $100,000 per year in the United States. Some patients have to accept the inevitability of death. Dr. Hagop Kantarjian at the MD Anderson Cancer Center reflected on the state of cancer health care in the U.S.: "People are abandoning treatment. People are scared they will go bankrupt and they will take away from family necessities and have to choose between treatment to prolong life or spend money on their family."

Girshriela Green, a mother of three girls, worked at Wal-Mart in Los Angeles in 2009 for $8.20 per hour. She mixed paint, cut keys, cut fabric, cashiered, and even unloaded trucks, but she was considered a part-time associate, and as a result had no benefits, and had to depend on public money for health care. She hurt her shoulder on the job, but was ignored by management. Without care, her condition worsened. She was eventually told she needed neck surgery.

Girshriela lived on $511 from worker's comp every two weeks, often going hungry to make sure her kids could eat. She couldn't afford the bus fare that would allow her youngest daughter to ride safely to school.

From Reno, Nevada: *Here I am at an age when I should be thinking about retiring, desperately trying to find a job. I have used my savings...I'm seeking a court injunction to try and save my home.*

From Bend, Oregon: *I exhausted all my 401(k) retirement savings...I'm one month away from losing everything and am now on Food Stamps. I'm an unhappy Republican...*

In Detroit, Michigan: 74-year-old Willie Smith saw her monthly SNAP benefits cut from $73 to $57. Also in Detroit, 63-year-old J.B. Hillman-Rushell and her 83-year-old mother were going to four different church food pantries for nearly all of their food.

## Notes

1 "Influenza 1918." *American Experience*, Public Broadcasting System; "March 4 1918—The First Case of Spanish Flu is Reported at Fort Riley, Kansas." Maps of the World; "Flu Epidemic of 1918." *Kansapedia*, Kansas Historical Society; "4th March 1918—Spanish flu begins." *This Day Then*.
2 "The Polio Crusade." *American Experience*, Public Broadcasting System; "Children receive first polio vaccine." *This Day in History*; "1955 Polio Vaccine Trial Announcement." School of Public Health, University of Michigan; "When polio vaccine backfired." *SFGate*, April 25, 2005.
3 "1955 Polio Vaccine Trial Announcement." School of Public Health, University of Michigan.
4 Buchheit, Paul, "Private Health Care as an Act of Terrorism." CommonDreams.org, July 20, 2015.
5 Case, Anne and Deaton, Angus, "Rising Morbidity and Mortality in Midlife among White Non-Hispanic Americans in the 21st century." Proceedings of the National Academy of Sciences, September 17, 2015.
6 "The Growing Gap in Life Expectancy by Income." National Academies of Sciences, Engineering, and Medicine, 2015.
7 "Definitions of Terrorism in the U.S. Code." *Federal Bureau of Investigation*.
8 "2015 Milliman Medical Index." *Milliman*, May 19, 2015.
9 Munro, Dan, "U.S. Healthcare Spending On Track to Hit $10,000 Per Person This Year." Forbes, January 4, 2015.
10 Graham, David A., "The True Face of Medicare Fraud." *The Atlantic*, June 19, 2015.
11 Johnson, Carolyn Y., "Specialty Drugs Now Cost More than the Median Household Income." *Washington Post*, November 20, 2015.
12 "Numbers of Americans Affected by Mental Illness." National Alliance on Mental Illness.

13  "State Mental Health Cuts: The Continuing Crisis." National Alliance on Mental Illness, November 2011.

14  "Nearly One in Five Adult Americans Experienced Mental Illness in 2013." The Substance Abuse and Mental Health Services Administration, November 20, 2014.

15  "Report to Congress on the Nation's Substance Abuse and Mental Health Workforce Issues." The Substance Abuse and Mental Health Services Administration, January 24, 2013.

16  "The Treatment of Persons with Mental Illness in Prisons and Jails: A State Survey." Treatment Advocacy Center and National Sheriff's Association, April 8, 2014.

17  Bai, Ge and Anderson, Gerald F., "Extreme Markup: the Fifty US Hospitals with the Highest Charge-To-Cost Ratios." *Health Affairs*, June 24, 2015.

18  Sifferlin, Alexandra, "Drug-Price Hikes." *Time*, September 24, 2015; Pollack, Andrew, "Martin Shkreli's Arrest Gives Drug-Makers Cover." *New York Times*, December 17, 2015.

19  Sun, Lena H., "50 Hospitals Charge Uninsured More than 10 Times Cost of Care, Study Finds." *Washington Post*, June 8, 2015.

20  Kristof, Nicholas, "An Idiot's Guide to Inequality." *New York Times*, July 23, 2014.

21  Stratmann, Thomas and Sheth, Darpana M., "Health Care Cartels Limit Americans' Options." *USA Today*, October 14, 2014.

22  Wilper, Andrew P., MD, "Health Insurance and Mortality in US Adults." *American Journal of Public Health*, December 2009.

23  "Compilation of Research from 200 Studies on the Correlation between Financial Stress and Health Care Costs." Financial Finesse, Inc. March 2011.

24  Artiga, Samantha; Damico, Anthony; Garfield, Rachel: "The Impact of the Coverage Gap for Adults in States Not Expanding Medicaid by Race and Ethnicity." Kaiser Family Foundation, October 26, 2015.

25  "Privately Insured in America: Opinions On Health Care Costs and Coverage." NORC Center for Public Affairs Research, The Associated Press.

26  "43 Percent of U.S. Working-Age Adults Can't Afford Doctor." UPI, April 26, 2013.

27  Gabler, Neal, "The Secret Shame of Middle-Class Americans." *The Atlantic*, May 2016 "What Resources Do Families Have for Financial Emergencies?" Pew Charitable Trusts, November 18, 2015; Morath, Eric, "Most Americans Don't Have Savings to Pay Unexpected Bill." *Wall Street Journal*, January 7, 2015.

28  Ingraham, Christopher, "Americans are Drinking Themselves to Death at Record Rates." *Washington Post*, December 22, 2015.

29  Ivory, Danielle; Protess, Ben; Bennett, Kitty: "When You Dial 911 and Wall Street Answers." *New York Times*, June 25, 2016.

30  Dickman, Samuel L.; Woolhandler, Steffie; Bor, Jacob; McCormick, Danny; Bor, David H.; Himmelstein, David U., "Health Spending for Low-, Middle-, And High-Income Americans, 1963–2012." *Health Affairs*, July 2016; "Wealthier Americans Now Get Much More Health Care than Middle Class or Poor: Harvard study." *EurekAlert*, July 6, 2016.

31  Bernstein, Nina, "Chefs, Butlers, Marble Baths: Hospitals Vie for the Affluent." *New York Times*, January 21, 2012.

32  Prince, Russ Alan, "Concierge Medicine for The Super-Rich." Forbes, February 5, 2015.

33  Buchheit, Paul, "Discarding the Elderly." NationOfChange.org, June 1, 2015.
34  Siedle, Edward, "The Greatest Retirement Crisis in American History." Forbes, March 20, 2013.
35  "Retirement Security: Most Households Approaching Retirement Have Low Savings." Government Accountability Office, June 2, 2015.
36  Kennedy, Bruce, "Shocking Number of Americans Have no Retirement Savings." *CBS Money Watch*, August 18, 2014.
37  "Late-Life Economic Inequality Has Risen Sharply in Recent Decades, Rutgers Study Finds." *Rutgers Today*, March 30, 2016.
38  "Economic Security for Seniors: Facts." National Council on Aging.
39  "Insight Report, Summary and Methodology." Global Age Watch, 2013, 2015.
40  Van de Water, Paul N. and Sherman, Arloc, "Social Security Keeps 20 Million Americans Out of Poverty." Center on Budget and Policy Priorities, August 11, 2010.
41  Steuerle, C. Eugene and Quakenbush, Caleb, "Social Security and Medicare Taxes and Benefits over a Lifetime." Urban Institute, 2012.
42  Jones, Jeffrey M., "More U.S. Nonretirees Expect to Rely on Social Security." Gallup, April 29, 2015.
43  Cecere, David, "New Study Finds 45,000 Deaths Annually Linked to Lack of Health Coverage." *Harvard Gazette*, September 17, 2009.
44  "Financial Wellness and Health Care Costs," Financial Finesse, March 2011; Johan P. Mackenbach, "Only the Poor Die Young." Project Syndicate, June 17, 2013; "The Growing Gap in Life Expectancy by Income." National Academies of Sciences, Engineering, and Medicine, 2015; Bosworth, Barry, Burtless, Gary, and Zhang, Kan, "The Growing Gap in Longevity between Rich and Poor and its Impact on Redistribution through Social Security." The Brookings Institution, 2016; Chetty, Raj; Stepner, Michael; Abraham, Sarah; Lin, Shelby; Scuderi, Benjamin; Turner, Nicholas; Bergeron, Augustin; Cutler, David: "The Association Between Income and Life Expectancy in the United States, 2001–2014." *Journal of the American Medical Association*, April 10, 2016.
45  Culp-Ressler, Tara, "The U.S. Is in 'Mediocre' Health, Falling Far Behind Other Wealthy Nations." *Think Progress*, July 10, 2013.
46  Skillern, Tim, "Going Hungry in America: 'Distressing,' 'Humbling' and 'Scary.'" Yahoo! News, August 22, 2012.
47  "Asking for Help at 80—America's New Faces of Hunger." PBS *News Hour*, May 22, 2015; Oksman, Olga, "How Crowdfunding Became a Lifeline for Cancer Patients Struggling with Debt." *The Guardian*, December 26, 2015; Abramsky, Sasha, Interviewer, "Girshriela Green." Voices of Poverty, December 13, 2011; "Voices of the Unemployed." Center for Effective Government, Story Archive; "Five Personal Stories of Food Insecurity in Metropolitan Detroit." Fair Food Network and Gleaners Community Food Bank, 2014.

## Bibliography

Marmot, Michael, *The Health Gap: The Challenge of an Unequal World*. Bloomsbury Press, 2015.
Wilkinson, Richard and Pickett, Kate, *The Spirit Level: Why Greater Equality Makes Societies Stronger*. Bloomsbury Press, 2009.

# 9

# EXTREME CAPITALISM

## Preying on the Sick and Retirees

Broadcast Journalist Edward R. Murrow in 1955: *Who owns the patent on this vaccine?*

Polio Researcher Jonas Salk: *Well, the people, I would say. There is no patent. Could you patent the sun?*

Pharmaceutical companies[1] reap billions of dollars in subsidies for research and development, but, as discussed earlier, they've successfully lobbied Congress to keep Medicare from bargaining for lower drug prices, and they pay competitors to keep generic drugs out of the market, to ensure that their more expensive drugs are the only option. Meanwhile, stunningly, for every $1 they spend on basic research, they invest $19 in promotion and marketing.[2] The industry has also cut nearly 150,000 jobs since 2008, mostly in R&D.[3]

Big firms use intellectual property law (another gift from the taxpayers) to snatch up patents on any new money-making products, no matter how much government- and university-funded research went into it. An example is genetically engineered insulin,[4] which due to patent protection cannot be made generically, and as a result can cost a patient up to $5,000 a year, about ten times more than a patent-expired version.

Pfizer deserves special attention. The company had *nearly half of its sales in the U.S.* over the past three years, yet *claimed losses in the U.S.* along with $50 billion in foreign profits. Despite paying an effective tax rate of just 7.5 percent in 2014, and despite being one of the nine pharmaceutical companies among the top 30 Fortune 500 firms in offshore tax hoarding,[5] Pfizer CEO Ian Read complained that U.S. taxes had his company fighting "with one hand tied behind our back."[6]

Pfizer has been spending everything on itself. From 2001 to 2015 the company spent an astounding 117 percent (!) of its income on investor-enriching stock buybacks and dividends,[7] while slashing its post-recession employee base from 110,000 to 78,000. To support its self-serving buyback obsession, Pfizer, along with other pharmaceutical companies, charges up to $10,000 per month for cancer drugs, an amount approximately 600 times the cost of production, and up to ten times higher than just 15 years ago.[8]

## Finance

Retirees are particularly impacted by the non-productive financial industry. Interest charged by private banks claims one out of every three dollars that we spend, and by the time we retire with a 401(k), over half of our money can be lost to the banks.[9] Even business-minded Forbes admitted, "…The great 401k experiment of the past 30 years has been a disaster. It is now apparent that 401ks will not provide the retirement security promised to workers."[10] Yet since 1983, thanks to the demise of company pensions, the number of private sector workers depending on a 401(k) instead of a company pension has increased from 12 percent to 68 percent.[11]

The financial industry exhibits a disregard for the fundamental economic needs of people, here and around the world, with companies like Goldman Sachs, whose commodities index is the most heavily traded in the world, hoarding rice, wheat, corn, sugar and livestock to jack up commodity prices around the globe, leaving poor families unable to afford basic staples.[12] Meanwhile, trading firms have fine-tuned their deal-making to the point that one company, Virtu Financial, made money in the stock market on 1,277 out of 1,278 days over a five-year period. Only one bad day in five years.[13]

A few decades ago, the financial industry spent most of its money on business investment. Today, most of it is being used for lending against existing assets such as housing, stocks and bonds. Despite generating about 25 percent of all corporate profits, it creates only about 4 percent of all jobs, while focusing on the short-term gains of investors rather than on productive long-term growth.[14]

And, of course, it focuses on annual bonuses, over and above salaries, adding up to enough money to boost all 2.6 million U.S. fast-food workers to a $15 minimum wage.[15]

The top 25 hedge fund managers made an average of a half-billion dollars each in 2015, even though hedge funds lost money for their investors in 2015, and are still losing in 2016.[16] A rigged financial system allows the hedge fund managers to pay much lower taxes by giving their income the magically deceptive name of "carried interest."[17]

A special case is the Chicago Mercantile Exchange (CME), where trading volume reached an incomprehensible $1 quadrillion in notional value in 2012.[18] That's a thousand trillion dollars, about three times more than the world's total wealth.[19] On that quadrillion dollars of sales, CME imposes transfer fees, contract fees, brokerage fees, Globex fees, clearing fees, and contract surcharges—many of them on both the buyer's and seller's side—and as a result, the company built up a profit margin higher than any of the other top 100 companies in the nation. But *not a penny in sales tax* was paid on these billions of financial transactions. Instead—unfathomably—CME complained that its taxes were too high, and they demanded and received an $85 million tax break from the State of Illinois.[20]

## Extreme Corporatization

A US Uncut report[21] calculated that annual subsidies to the oil, agriculture, pharmaceutical, and banking industries is $1.5 trillion per year, *ten times more* than the three main safety net programs: Temporary Assistance for Needy Families, food stamps, and the Earned Income Tax Credit.

Even though corporate profits are at their highest level in 85 years,[22] corporations aren't creating many middle-class jobs. Like Pfizer and Walmart and the financial industry, they're widening the management/labor disparity. In 2014, S&P companies spent 95 percent of their profits on stock buybacks to enrich executives and shareholders.[23] Exxon and Apple are the latest big companies to demonstrate a short-term eagerness to pump up stock prices rather than factories and jobs.[24]

Declining earnings have finally begun to curtail the buyback frenzy.[25]

As for the $2 trillion in cash being held tax-free overseas, according to the *Wall Street Journal*, over 75 percent of the money hoarded by some of our largest corporations is actually kept "at U.S. banks, held in U.S. dollars or parked in U.S. government and corporate securities."[26] Researcher Gabriel Zucman estimates that tax havens hide $7.6 trillion—remarkably, about eight percent of the world's net financial wealth.[27]

Corporate *inversions*[28] encourage companies to save taxes by moving their corporate offices to foreign countries, where they can merge with "parent" companies, thus effectively *deserting the country* that made them successful. The betrayal gets worse. Some inverted firms "borrow" money from their own parent company, using the tax-deductible interest payments to offset taxable profits. The company is *borrowing from itself* to skip out on taxes.[29]

A 2013 Government Accountability Office study found that profitable U.S. corporations paid U.S. federal income taxes amounting to about 13 percent of their pretax worldwide income.[30] The unpaid taxes of just 500 companies could pay for a job for every unemployed American, for two years, at the nation's median salary of $36,000, for all eight million unemployed people.

Oxfam estimates that from 2008 to 2014, the 50 largest U.S. companies collectively received approximately *$27 in government support for every $1 they paid* in federal taxes.[31]

Between 70 percent and 90 percent of the 1.6 million corporations in the U.S. pay no income tax at all.[32]

But as wealthy conservatives devise new tax avoidance strategies, they are actually pushing a bill that would *excuse corporate leaders from financial fraud*, environmental pollution, and other crimes that America's business elite deem simply reckless or negligent.[33] The Heritage Foundation attempts to rationalize, saying "someone who simply has an accident by being slightly careless can hardly be said to have acted with a 'guilty mind.'"

One must wonder, then, what degrees of guilt led to criminal charges against people apparently *aware of their actions*: the Ohio woman who took coins from a fountain to buy food; the California man who broke into a church kitchen to find something to eat; and the 90-year-old Florida activist who tried to feed the homeless.[34]

Of course, even without the explicit protection of Congress, CEOs are rarely charged for their crimes. Not a single Wall Street executive faced prosecution for the fraud-ridden 2008 financial crisis.

## Oil

On February 14, 2011 an Ecuadorean judge ruled that oil giant Chevron was responsible for the pollution of the country's jungle in the 1970s and 1980s.[35] He ordered the company to pay more than $9 billion in damages. The plaintiffs, who were seeking over $100 billion, nevertheless called the ruling a "triumph of justice," although it's unlikely that Chevron will pay up any time soon, if at all. A Chevron spokesman called the decision "illegitimate and unenforceable."

On October 28, 2005 the Chevron Texaco Company held a gala ceremony to present the annual Chevron Conservation Awards, recognizing the employees who have "helped to protect wildlife, restore wilderness, create natural preserves and parks, and institute educational programs to heighten environmental awareness."[36]

In 2001, Condoleezza Rice, who was on the Chevron Board of Directors in 1998, told Fox News: "I think we should be very proud of the job that American oil companies are doing in exploration abroad..."[37]

In recent years, Exxon and Chevron, with over 75 percent of their productive oil and gas wells in the U.S., both declared less than 20 percent of their income here.[38] Exxon paid less than two percent of its total income in current U.S. taxes, Chevron less than one percent. As if to mock the tax system, Exxon used a *theoretical tax* to account for 83 percent of their smallish 2014 income tax bill. Yet royalties charged to the oil and gas companies by the U.S. government are among the lowest in the world.[39]

## Technology

The tech industry, like Big Pharma, has long depended on public money, which even today still makes up 57 percent of basic research.[40] Robert Reich points out the stifling monopolies surrounding Google's search engine, Amazon's shopping system, and Facebook's social networking platform.[41] Only two or three companies make phones. Same with computer operating systems. With little competition to impede them, by 2012 Apple and Google were spending more on patent purchases and lawsuits than on research and development.[42]

## Automotive

The auto industry is another example of the placement of profit over the common good and, as in the pharmaceutical industry, over public health. Even as General Motors was accepting billions in bailout funds, it was knowingly subjecting customers to deadly ignition switch failures.[43] Volkswagen cheated millions of customers, deceiving them with supposedly clean-running diesel engines that were, in fact, equipped with special mechanisms to fool the pollution testers. Top management blamed the technicians. Despite the malfeasance, Volkswagen recently received nearly $1 billion in subsidies from the taxpayers of Tennessee.[44]

## Walmart

Then there's Walmart.[45] In addition to the company's $19 billion in U.S. profits in one recent year, the four Walton siblings together made about $29 billion from their personal investments. That's over $33,000 per U.S. Walmart employee in profits and family stock gains. Yet they pay their 1.4 million American employees so little that the average Walmart worker depends on about $4,000 per year in taxpayer assistance, for food stamps and other safety net programs.[46]

How does Walmart spend its profits? Instead of providing a living wage for its workers, company management spent $7.6 billion, or about $5,000 per U.S. employee, on stock buybacks to further boost the value of their stock holdings.[47]

## Notes

1   Sweetland Edwards, Haley, "Why Can't Drug Costs Be Reined in?" *Time*, May 19, 2016.
2   "Pharmaceutical Research and Development: What Do we Get for All That Money?" *BMJ* 2012, 345: e4348.
3   Foroohar, Rana, "Too Many Businesses Want a Piece of the Financial Action." *Financial Times*, May 15, 2016.
4   Rosenthal, Elisabeth, "Even Small Medical Advances Can Mean Big Jumps in Bills." *New York Times*, April 5, 2014; Gordon, Serena, "How Drug Companies Keep Insulin

Prices High." CBS News, March 19, 2015; von Wartburg, Linda, "Why Does Insulin Cost More Than Ever? It's All in The Way It's Made." *Diabetes Health*, July 27, 2009.

5   "Pfizer's Tax Dodging Rx: Stash Profits Offshore." Americans for Tax Fairness, November 2015; "Offshore Shell Games 2015." Citizens for Tax Justice, October 5, 2015.

6   Colvin, Geoff, "Pfizer's CEO Isn't a Hero or a Villain." *Fortune*, November 25, 2015.

7   Lazonick, William, "Tax Dodging Just One Part of Pfizer's Corrupt Business Model." *Huffington Post*, December 6, 2015.

8   "In Support of a Patient-Driven Initiative and Petition to Lower the High Price of Cancer Drugs." Mayo Clinic Proceedings, August 2015.

9   "The Retirement Gamble." *Frontline*, April 23, 2013.

10   Siedle, Edward, "The Greatest Retirement Crisis in American History." *Forbes*, March 20, 2013.

11   "Workers with Pension Coverage." *Center for Retirement Research at Boston College*, February 2013.

12   Doane, Deborah, "What Goldman Sachs Should Admit: It Drives Up the Cost of Food." *The Guardian*, May 23, 2013.

13   de la Merced, Michael J. and Alden, William, "Scrutiny for Wall Street's Warp Speed." *New York Times*, March 31, 2014.

14   Foroohar, Rana, *Makers and Takers: The Rise of Finance and the Fall of American Business*. Penguin Random House, 2016; Foroohar, Rana, "American Capitalism's Great Crisis." *Time*, May 23, 2016.

15   Chang, Sue, "Wall Street's $25 Bln Bonus Isn't Pretty in Minimum-Wage Context." *Market Watch*, March 8, 2016.

16   Herbst-Bayliss, Svea, "Best-Paid U.S. Hedge Fund Managers Take Home $13 Billion." Reuters, May 10, 2016; "A Losing Bet: Hedge Funds Haven't Delivered on Their Promise." *The Economist*, May 7, 2016.

17   Lewis Mernit, Judith, "How the Hedge Fund Billionaires Get Away with Obscene Tax Avoidance." *Alternet*, June 21, 2016; Patricof, Alan J., "Close My Tax Loophole." *New York Times*, August 26, 2016.

18   *2012 Annual Report*, CME Group.

19   "Global Wealth Databook 2015." Credit Suisse, October 2015.

20   Buchheit, Paul, "Chicago for Sale." CommonDreams.org, February 2, 2015.

21   Cahill, Tom, "10 Taxpayer Handouts to the Super Rich That Will Make Your Blood Boil." *US Uncut*, October 28, 2015.

22   Norris, Floyd, "Corporate Profits Grow and Wages Slide." *New York Times*, April 4, 2014.

23   Wang, Lu and Bost, Callie, "S&P 500 Companies Spend Almost All Profits on Buybacks." Bloomberg Business, October 6, 2014.

24   Foroohar, Rana, "The Sad Truth That Apple and Exxon Reveal About Our Economy." *Time*, April 27, 2016; Mason, J.W., "Disgorge the Cash: The Disconnect Between Corporate Borrowing and Investment." The Roosevelt Institute, February 25, 2015.

25   Saft, James, "The Great Stock Buyback Boom Is Over." Reuters, August 30, 2016.

26   Linebaugh, Kate, "Firms Keep Stockpiles of 'Foreign' Cash in U.S." *Wall Street Journal*, January 22, 2013.

27 Drucker, Jesse, "If You See a Little Piketty in This Tax-Haven Book, That's Fine." *Bloomberg BusinessWeek*, September 21, 2015.

28 Dickinson, Tim, "The Biggest Tax Scam Ever." *Rolling Stone*, August 27, 2014; Humer, Caroline and Pierson, Ransdell, "Obama's Inversion Curbs Kill Pfizer's $160 Billion Allergan Deal." Reuters, April 6, 2016.

29 Solomon, Steven Davidoff, "Corporate Inversions Aren't the Half of It." *New York Times*, February 10, 2016.

30 "Corporate Income Tax: Effective Tax Rates Can Differ Significantly from the Statutory Rate." Government Accountability Office, May 20, 2013.

31 "Fifty Biggest Global US Companies Stash $1.3 Trillion Offshore." Oxfam, April 14, 2016.

32 Ehrenfreund, Max, "Thanks to Bernie Sanders, We Now Know How Many Big Corporations Don't Pay Taxes." *Washington Post*, April 16, 2016; Worstall, Tim, "More Than 90% of US Businesses Don't Pay the Corporate Income Tax." Forbes, December 23, 2014.

33 Carter, Zach, "House Bill Would Make It Harder to Prosecute White-Collar Crime." *Huffington Post*, November 16, 2015.

34 Einenkel, Walter, "90 Year Old Activist Arrested Again for Feeding the Homeless in Florida." *Daily Kos*, November 6, 2014.

35 Romero, Simon and Krauss, Clifford, "Ecuador Judge Orders Chevron to Pay $9 Billion." *New York Times*, February 14, 2011.

36 Herbert, Bob, "Rain Forest Jekyll and Hyde?" *New York Times*, October 20, 2005.

37 Goodman, Amy, *Exception to the Rulers*. Haymarket Books, 2008.

38 SEC Company Filings (www.sec.gov/edgar/searchedgar/companysearch.html), accessed May 31, 2016.

39 Gentile, Nicole, "Federal Oil and Gas Royalty and Revenue Reform." Center for American Progress, June 19, 2015.

40 "The Pivotal Role of Government Investment in Basic Research." U.S. Congress Joint Economic Committee, May 2010.

41 Reich, Robert, *Saving Capitalism: For the Many, Not the Few*. Knopf, 2015.

42 House, Morgan, "100 Startling Facts About the Economy." *Motley Fool*, February 5, 2013.

43 Uhlmann, David M., "Justice Falls Short in G.M. Case." *New York Times*, September 19, 2015.

44 Mattera, Philip and Tarczynska, Kasia with LeRoy, Greg, "Megadeals." GoodJobsFirst.org, June 2013.

45 SEC Company Filings (www.sec.gov/edgar/searchedgar/companysearch.html), accessed May 31, 2016.

46 "Walmart on Tax Day." Americans for Tax Fairness, April 2014.

47 Ruetschlin, Catherine and Traub, Amy, "A Higher Wage is Possible." Demos.org, November 2013.

## Bibliography

Alperovitz, Gar, *What Then Must We Do?: Straight Talk about the Next American Revolution*. Chelsea Green, 2013.

Anderson, Irvine, *Aramco, the United States, and Saudi Arabia*. Princeton Press, 1981.

Beaud, Michel, *A History of Capitalism, 1500–2000*. Monthly Review Press, 2002.

Collins, Chuck, *Born on Third Base: A One-Percenter Makes the Case for Tackling Inequality, Bringing Wealth Home, and Investing in the Common Good*. Chelsea Green, 2016.

Derber, Charles and Magrass, Yale R., *Bully Nation*. University Press of Kansas, 2016.

Foroohar, Rana, *Makers and Takers: The Rise of Finance and the Fall of American Business*. Penguin Random House, 2016.

Frank, Robert, *Richistan: A Journey Through the American Wealth Boom and the Lives of the New Rich*. Crown, 2007.

Freeland, Chrystia, *Plutocrats: The Rise of the New Global Super-Rich and the Fall of Everyone Else*. Penguin, 2012.

Goodman, Amy, *Exception to the Rulers*. Haymarket Books, 2008.

Hartmann, Thom, *Unequal Protection: The Rise of Corporate Dominance and the Theft of Human Rights*. Rodale, 2004.

Hartmann, Thom, *Crash of 2016*. Twelve, 2013.

Leopold, Les, *The Looting of America: How Wall Street's Game of Fantasy Finance Destroyed Our Jobs, Pensions, and Prosperity*. Chelsea Green Publishing, 2009.

Leopold, Les, *Runaway Inequality: An Activist's Guide to Economic Justice*. Labor Institute Press, 2015.

Mayer, Jane, *Dark Money: The Hidden History of the Billionaires Behind the Rise of the Radical Right*. Random House Audio, 2016.

McQuaig, Linda and Brooks, Neil, *Billionaires' Ball: Gluttony and Hubris in an Age of Epic Inequality*. Beacon Press, 2012.

Miller, Aaron David, *Search for Security*. North Carolina Press, 1991.

Palast, Greg, *The Best Democracy Money Can Buy*. Plume, 2004.

Patnaik, Prabhat, *Capitalism and Its Current Crisis*. Monthly Review Press, 2016.

Perkins, John, *The New Confessions of an Economic Hit Man*. Berrett-Koehler, 2016.

Pizzigati, Sam, *The Rich Don't Always Win: The Forgotten Triumph over Plutocracy that Created the American Middle Class, 1900–1970*. Seven Stories Press, 2012.

Stoff, Michael B., *Oil, War, and American Security*. Yale University Press, 1982.

Zucman, Gabriel, *The Hidden Wealth of Nations: The Scourge of Tax Havens*. University of Chicago Press, 2015.

# 10
## YOUTH

## The Past: Depression-Era Youth[1]

**FIGURE 10.1** Two hobos walking along railroad tracks, after being put off a train.
Library of Congress (https://commons.wikimedia.org/wiki/File:Hobos.jpg).

**FIGURE 10.2** Lou Ambers with a large bag over his shoulder, mounting the ladder of a train car.
Library of Congress: Alan Fisher, photographer (www.loc.gov/pictures/item/2001696792/).

Sixteen-year-old Jim Mitchell left his home in Wisconsin in 1933. "I remember... My dad came home and it seemed strange. The first time in my life I ever saw my father cry. And he said, 'I lost my job.'"

Nineteen-year-old Californian Charley Bull described the ordeal of hopping a freight: "You're running along and trying to match your speed with the speed of the train and you get a hand-hold here first and you swing yourself around and you're still running and you get two hand-holds. Then is the first time you lift your foot...You could ride on top of a freight car and then you just had to be careful. If a train is going sixty or seventy miles an hour and hits a curve and you're walking and your back's to the turn and you don't see it coming—a little tiny turn can throw you right off the train. A lot of people have been killed like that, they don't know."

John Fawcett, who was 16 when he left West Virginia, remembered his first train ride: "The train hadn't even stopped, and there was a gun and a flashlight in my face, right up there in the blinds...This is at midnight. And in ten minutes, why, we were behind bars."

During the Great Depression, a quarter-million teenagers were living as runaways, hobos, hitch-hikers, adventurers. There was no reason to stay at home, with their families destitute, often evicted from their homes. Many parents were telling their children they couldn't support them anymore.

Kids hopped the trains, and went to strange towns where they might find a mission or a Salvation Army center. For a meal and a bed, 16-year-olds would sit through a sermon. Some chose instead to rely on the kindliness of farmers for a meal. Clarence Lee, an African-American, who left his Louisiana home at the age of 16, remarked: "If they was white kids, they fared better...They might let them stay in a house with them, but me, I could sleep in a barn with the mules and hay."

Other young people stayed in the "jungles," camps set up on the outskirts of towns, usually in a grove of trees, removed from sight of the townspeople. "There's residents in there, old jungle buzzards as we used to call them, that lived there for weeks or months at a time."

Some went all the way west, to the California growing fields. "Whitey" Symmonds remembered, "It was all Okies, Arkies, Texans, and whoever, you know. We'd start in strawberries and work clear on through apples, and beans, hoeing hops, all kinds of things 'til potatoes in the fall down in Tule Lake, California, and end up shaking walnuts." But because of the Depression, prices were so low that many of the crops were almost worthless. "Once I worked for man who wanted me to unload a coal car. I stood up there and threw down the coal. I worked all day. He gave me two tomatoes."

## *Jobs: the Civilian Conservation Corps[2]*

**FIGURE 10.3** CCC enrollees help to control the Malibu fire near Angeles, CA.
U.S. Forest Service: Gerald W. Williams Collection (https://commons.wikimedia.org/wiki/File:CCC_enrollees_help_to_control_the_Malibu_fire_near_Angeles_National_Forest,_California_(3226886348).jpg).

**FIGURE 10.4** Civilian Conservation Corps in Sequoia National Park, California.
National Archives: Franklin D. Roosevelt Library Public Domain Photographs (https://commons.
wikimedia.org/wiki/File:Civilian_Conservation_Corps_in_California,_Camp_Wolverton,_
Sequoia_National_Park_-_NARA_-_197077.tif).

Harley Jolley, joined the CCC in 1937: *We had not taken care of our land…
Part of it goes back to the big timber companies of the '20s and '30s, cutting and
cutting and cutting, leaving slash. Slash would burn, storms would come, floods
would come, and down the river goes our good fertile soil.*

Jonathan Alter, writer: *[Franklin] Roosevelt believed that work was ultimately
more important than relief…The CCC was a win–win for FDR. Both put
hundreds of thousands, eventually millions of people to work. And he also did
something for posterity, for future generations, for what we would now call the
Environment.*

Houston Pritchett, joined the CCC in 1939: *You get out there in that hot sun,
it's 100 degrees, and you're working all day. And you sweatin'. And you worked
right up to lunchtime. Then they bring you food out to the field…We wasn't used
to nothing like this.*

Vicente Ximenes, joined the CCC in 1938: *Even in my own camp, there
were individuals who were outright racists, you know, to individuals who were the
recipients of racism. I learned that we could get both sides to come together…*

Clifford Hammond, joined the CCC in 1934: *I used to think I was better than a Mexican because there's no Mexicans in Illinois when I was growing up, you know. All the farm boys and girls just all white like me...they're just like anybody else.*

## The Present: The Struggles of Young Adults[3]

Just before the year 2000, a quarter of all 25-year-olds lived at home with their parents.[4] Today, half of them live with their parents or another supporting family member.[5] The average debt of 25- to 34-year-olds is five times higher than just 15 years ago.[6]

## *Higher Education: Capitalism at Its Worst*

Rating industry wrongdoing is a daunting task, with Big Pharma and High Finance in the running, but Higher Ed's betrayal of a century-old trust with young Americans vaults it toward the top of the list.

Since 1862, public colleges had been expected to serve primarily as a means for the American people to achieve an inexpensive college education, and to benefit from academic research. The 1980 Bayh-Dole Act changed it all.[7] It freed public universities from releasing new research discoveries to the public, allowing them instead to patent the results and make licensing deals with private companies. The University of California, anticipating big agri-business subsidies, took full advantage in 2013, siding with Monsanto in a lawsuit against a farmer who was accused of stealing the company's seed by replanting the seed the year after purchase. The farmer lost. And universities became more deeply entrenched in the capitalist world.[8]

There are other reasons for the continuing degradation of higher education:

## *The Rise of the All-Administrative University*

That's the subtitle of a 2011 book[9] by Benjamin Ginsberg, who noted that administrators nearly doubled their numbers in twenty years while increasing their staff by 240 percent. That staff includes deanlets and deputies, provosts and vice-provosts, directors of communications and diversity and development, and various assistants and assistants to the assistants.

The National Center for Education Statistics reported that "For every $1 spent on instruction, $1.82 is spent on non-instructional things such as 'academic support, student services, institutional support, public service' and a catch-all category called 'other.'"[10]

As administrators grew at ten times the rate of tenured faculty positions,[11] much of the redirected money has gone for amenities like recreation centers, dining halls, and athletic centers.[12] At New York University, condos and vacation homes were part of the package for administrators and business faculty.[13] The city areas around elite tax-exempt universities are often filled with potholes and boarded-up houses due to the lack of property tax income.

To ensure that they get their way, institutions of higher learning have employed a massive lobbying force in Washington, topping all industries except pharmaceuticals and technology.[14]

## The Coming of the "All-Adjunct" University

The state of higher-ed teaching in America: Years of study by trusting young scholars who end up with academic positions that pay as much as entry-level fast-food jobs.[15]

Adjuncts made up less than a quarter of instructional staff in 1969, but now make up over three-quarters of instructors. They make a median wage of about $2,700 per course, with little or no benefits.[16]

Many adjunct teachers are on food stamps.[17] Some are homeless. Yet over 90 percent of adjuncts responding to a House Democrats survey had advanced degrees.[18]

## Tuition Shock: 12 Times More Than Your Parents Paid

Older Americans can remember working summer jobs to pay their tuition.

Tuition has increased by over 1,000 percent since 1978 as revenue-deprived states have slashed higher education funding. The Consumer Price Index, according to *The Economist*, went from 100 to 400 since 1978, while tuition went from 100 to 1200.[19]

In 2012, undergraduates across the U.S. spent $62.6 billion on public college tuition.[20] Yet in 2013, the federal government spent $69 billion on financial aid programs, excluding loans.[21] A good argument for free tuition.

## Today's Jobs: Food Stamps on the Side

Older Americans can also remember graduating debt-free into their choice of jobs.

Today's hard-working students come out of college with tens of thousands of dollars in loans, unskilled jobs, garnished wages, and no legal way to declare bankruptcy.[22] As graduating students were entering the working world after the recession, almost 60 percent of the new jobs were low-income ($7.69 to $13.83 per hour).[23] The number of college grads working for minimum wage doubled in just five years.[24]

Older, established, and largely white male America has taken the greater part of our nation's wealth while deceiving college kids with dreams of success in an unregulated high-tech sharing economy. According to Pew Research, from 1984 to 2009, the net worth of an American under 35 dropped from $11,521 to $3,662 (down 68 percent), while for Americans over 65, it went up 42 percent.[25] Especially forsaken are Black and Hispanic graduates, who have actually seen their wealth fall *faster than less-educated* Blacks and Hispanics.[26]

The reality is that almost half[27] of recent college graduates are underemployed, working at the level of high-school graduates, after taking a 19 percent pay cut in the two years after the recession.[28]

## College Sports as Modern Minstrel Shows

According to a 2013 University of Pennsylvania study, black men were less than three percent of full-time undergrad students from 2007 to 2010, but made up 57 percent of football teams and 64 percent of basketball teams.[29] A University of Washington Law Review had concluded a few years earlier that the athlete–university relationship is "not primarily academic, but is, instead, undeniably commercial."[30] Yet the National Labor Relations Board ruled against Northwestern University football players who demanded union representation.[31]

Meanwhile, the big universities rake in the money, largely tax-free, from broadcast rights, luxury suites, seat donations, and advertising, and even more money from taxpayers in the form of stadium subsidies.[32] All the hundreds of millions of dollars have allowed universities to increase head football coach salaries at a rate 20 times that of college professors.[33]

Winner-take-all capitalism has taken over higher education. The winners are in the administrative offices.

## Philanthropy is Not the Answer

Decisions about higher education should be made by all of us, with public tax dollars allocated in a democratic fashion. But our tax dollars have gone away. The Reagan-era "government is the problem" attitude led to dramatic tax cuts and a resulting decline in government funding for public universities. Instead of paying for all the societal benefits heaped upon them, billionaires keep getting richer—just 14 individuals making more than the entire federal education budget two years in a row.

As a result, as noted by Larry Wittner,[34] "campus administrators, faced with declining income, are increasingly inclined to accept funding from wealthy individuals and corporations that are reshaping higher education to serve their interests." The Koch brothers have spent millions funding universities and stipulating the kind of education that should be provided.[35]

We're left with philanthropy instead of democracy. The philanthropists, not we the people, are beginning to make these vital decisions. Said Charles Koch: "I believe my business and non-profit investments are much more beneficial to societal well-being than sending more money to Washington."[36]

## Beyond the Universities: How Big Business Is Divesting Young Americans

In his early-2016 letter[37] to his Berkshire Hathaway stockholders, Warren Buffett, whose company has been deferring its taxes for years,[38] proclaimed: *The babies being born in America today are the luckiest crop in history...America's economic magic remains alive and well.*

A well-positioned segment of our country's once-idealistic baby boomer generation has victimized young adults entering the working world. A Small Business Administration study found that only two percent of the Millennial Generation are entrepreneurs (self-employed or business owners), compared to 6.7 percent of Baby Boomers and 5.4 percent in Generation X.[39] According to the Kauffman Foundation, 20- to 34-year-olds made up over a third of all new business startups in 1997, but less than a quarter of them today.[40] The super-rich have manipulated the financial system to the point that would-be entrepreneurs, many of them young and deeply in debt, are unable or unwilling to take chances on new startups.[41]

Yet on a *global scale*, youth entrepreneurship is *on the rise*. America is *exceptional* in its entrepreneurial decline.[42]

A small percentage of older Americans have taken almost all the new wealth since the recession.[43] From 2000 to 2012, corporations more than doubled their profits and halved their taxes. What have they been doing with all that money? Hoarding it, mostly. David Cay Johnston estimated that in 2013, American businesses held almost $7.9 trillion of liquid assets worldwide.[44]

As already noted, corporations are also spending trillions of dollars on *stock buybacks*, which use potential research and development money, and possibly job creation funds, to pump up the prices of executive stock options.[45] For every job created in the U.S. over the past ten years, U.S. corporations have spent $296,000 on stock buybacks.[46]

Meanwhile, corporations continue to cut jobs, with the computer industry among the worst offenders at the start of 2014. Microsoft recently announced the deepest cuts in the firm's 39-year history. AT&T has reduced its workforce by 22 percent in the last seven years. Verizon is shutting down customer service centers. Apple, one of the nation's biggest tax avoiders, defended its outsourcing, saying "We shouldn't be criticized for using Chinese workers. The U.S. has stopped producing people with the skills we need." Yet Apple undermines its American workers, earning $400,000 profit per employee[47] while paying most of their store workers $13 to $15 per hour.[48]

With a hint of condescension, the media looks down at a struggling class of young Americans and proclaims:

The good news is that information technology provides the iPod/Facebook generation with the means to find work and create careers.

Michael Barone, *Washington Examiner*[49]

A lot of people...can still earn a good living now by building their own branded reputations.

Thomas Friedman, *New York Times*[50]

The ability to so take photographs makes [people] richer.

Forbes[51]

But the truth has become clear in New York City, where millennials in 2014 earned about 20 percent less than their counterparts in the previous generation. Jobs in arts and entertainment, and in hospitality and food service and retail, have increased in numbers, but with a dramatic decline in wages. Meanwhile, fewer and fewer young adults have been able to find employment in the increasingly lucrative financial industry.[52]

## A Global Concern

The problem of youth underemployment is greatly magnified on the global stage, especially in poor countries, where young adult populations keep increasing while opportunities for living-wage jobs fail to keep up. Around the world, 40 percent of young people of working age are unemployed or underemployed.[53] That figure reaches an astounding 90 percent in low-income countries.[54] And in the Middle East and North Africa, growing populations of jobless youth are feeding the European immigration crisis, and adding numbers to the ranks of militant groups that thrive on the rebelliousness of dissatisfied young people.[55]

## The Personal Stories of Young People

### Taking Advantage of a Gifted Young Man

A *New York Times* report[56] chronicled the high school and college years of Keith Frazier, a talented basketball player who would bring prestige and profit to the adults responsible for his progress. The report was based on confidential information from Dallas high schools and the NCAA sanctions report on Southern Methodist University.

Until his junior year in 2011–12, Frazier had played high school basketball in Irving, Texas. Early in the season, his mother announced that because of rising rent costs they were moving to a Dallas apartment near Kimball High School, which was the reigning state basketball champion. A local investigative reporter later discovered that the federally subsidized rent charges in Irving had been set at $505 a month, and had not changed.

At Kimball, Frazier's grades mysteriously improved just before his evaluation for basketball eligibility, and with his dominant play the school earned a second consecutive state championship in 2012.

A year later, as Frazier developed into one of the nation's top players, Southern Methodist University coach Larry Brown, who had been enshrined in the Basketball Hall of Fame, despite scandals at both UCLA and Kansas, aggressively recruited the young star. He employed an SMU assistant coach to pressure Kimball into making the necessary grade adjustments for Frazier's college eligibility. Teachers refused to change grades. Yet, once again under a cloud of suspicion, Keith passed all his classes. After landing him, Brown proclaimed, "Keith changed our program... We've never been successful in recruiting inner-city kids."

In the summer of 2013, Dallas school investigators concluded that a "fraudulent report" had been sent to the college admissions office. Dallas school officials responded by firing Anita Connally, a former teacher who had investigated the grade-fixing. SMU officials waited well over a month to respond to a request for assistance, basically ignoring the allegations against Kimball, and dismissing objections from its own college faculty, who recommended that the basketball player be denied admission. SMU administrators overruled the teachers on the grounds of an "extraordinary exception" based on "the broader university perspective and needs."

The NCAA finally began its own investigation in January 2015. Brown received a nine-game suspension, and SMU—with one of the top records in the nation—was made ineligible for 2016 post-season play. Frazier lost his starting position. He stopped showing up for practice, and soon after, he left the university.

Larry Brown reflected: "We were all trying to help him. It's kind of a tragedy."

On the day the *New York Times* report was released, Keith Frazier was arrested after a fight in a bar.

### Student Loans[57]

"I wish I hadn't gone to school," says Mark, who graduated in 2005 with degrees in psychology and music and $875 monthly payments on $80,000 worth of student loans. "I had to claim bankruptcy...which of course did nothing to the student loans." (Student loan debt is nearly impossible to discharge through bankruptcy.)

At 23, Katie will start paying off her $40,000 student loan in September— with no job prospects on the horizon. "If I could turn back time I would consider not going to college," she says. "I could have started a job right away, worked my way up to management, and not be $40,000 in debt with interest growing every month."

"In just a few months, I'm going to turn 62 years old," says William, who took out $44,000 in private loans to study psychology. "I've been attempting to pay back my student loan debt for 22 years...I've worked at times four jobs to try to pay back the debt." He has paid back $31,000. He still has tens of thousands to pay off.

When Nick was denied federal student loans, he took out a $30,000 Smart Option loan from private lender Sallie Mae. "I'm in a spot where I can't pay it off," he says. "I literally lose sleep thinking about...if I didn't go to school, I'd probably be better off."

> I have never missed a payment in over ten years...To date, I have paid over $40,000 in loan payments...I now owe $15,000 more than I borrowed.
>
> Anonymous

After Jody Sofia's loans for a Florida law school surged from $92,000 to $144,000, calls from collection agencies became more frequent, and more aggressive. She couldn't pay. She had graduated, but was unable to find a job in a legal field, and had to resume her former occupation as an insurance adjuster. She wonders now about all the government money spent on private contractors for debt servicing, refinancing, and default advisors. "The government," she says, "is spending all this money for these people to constantly call you. How effective is that?"

Thirty-six-year-old Nick Keith graduated from the California Culinary Academy with about $60,000 in student loans, which eight years later had **ballooned to $142,000**. "My life," says Keith, "has become a daily swim in a tar pit with very little hope of ever getting out."

A love for healthy food and encouragement from the school's recruiters gave him high hopes early on. He anticipated 12 months of study with a three-month externship, and then, based on the school's claims, near-certain employment. He arranged for $46,000 in private loans and another $14,000 in federal loans to cover tuition and room and board.

His first job in the culinary field was on a $10/hour meal assembly line. It took three months to make the first payment of $1,300 on his private loan, which had a variable rate ranging up to a usurious 19 percent. Keith recalls, "My choice each month was to either pay my rent or make a student loan payment." Bankruptcy was out of the question, since the finance industry had convinced Congress that student loans, unlike other types of debt, cannot be relinquished. So he just stopped paying.

Then life got even more difficult for Nick Keith: he became permanently disabled after a work injury. He receives $1,200 per month in disability, supplements it by collecting cans and bottles, and goes to the food bank or Salvation Army for many of his meals. He lives out of his van, even though his credit score is too low to obtain car insurance. Most nights are passed at a truck stop. He is, for all practical purposes, homeless.

The California Culinary Academy admitted its role in defrauding students, and agreed to partially reimburse thousands of them. Keith stands to receive about $16,000—once the school's appeals have all been dismissed.

## Notes

1 "Riding the Rails." *American Experience*, Public Broadcasting System.
2 "The Civilian Conservation Corps." *American Experience*, Public Broadcasting System.
3 Buchheit, Paul, "Nine Numbers That Cry Out: 'Bring On Bernie!'" CommonDreams. org, December 21, 2015; Buchheit, Paul, "Higher Education: Capitalism at Its Most Despicable." CommonDreams.org, October 26, 2015; Buchheit, Paul, "Abuses that Wouldn't Exist in a Socialist America." NationOfChange.org, November 2, 2015; Buchheit, Paul, "How Capitalism Is Cheating Young Americans." Truthout Buzzflash, July 28, 2014.
4 "Why Are More Young Adults Still Living at Home?" *St. Louis Federal Reserve*, October 26, 2015.
5 Fry, Richard, "For First Time in Modern Era, Living with Parents Edges Out Other Living Arrangements for 18- to 34-Year-Olds." Pew Research Center, May 24, 2016.
6 *The Sightlines Project*, Stanford University, February 2016.
7 Rhines, Robert, "Consequences of the Bayh-Dole Act." MIT, December 12, 2005.
8 *Bowman v. Monsanto Co.*, 2013.
9 Ginsberg, Benjamin, *The Fall of the Faculty*. Oxford University Press, 2011.
10 Vedder, Richard, "As Tuition Increases, So Do College Bureaucracies." Bloomberg View, February 3, 2014.
11 Campos, Paul F., "The Real Reason College Tuition Costs So Much." *New York Times*, April 4, 2015.
12 "Colleges Are Buying Stuff They Can't Afford and Making Students Pay." *The Nation*, May 23, 2014.
13 "The Art of the Gouge." NYU Faculty against the Sexton Plan, March 23, 2012.
14 Mullins, Brody; Belkin, Douglas; Fuller, Andrea: "Colleges Flex Lobbying Muscle." *Wall Street Journal*, November 8, 2015.
15 "Part-Time Professors Demand Higher Pay; Will Colleges Listen?" National Public Radio, February 3, 2014.
16 "The Changing Academic Workforce." Association of Governing Boards, May/June 2013; DePillis, Lydia, "Adjunct Professors Get Poverty-Level Wages. Should Their Pay Quintuple?" *Washington Post*, February 6, 2015.
17 "The High Public Cost of Low Wages." *UC Berkeley Labor Center*, April 2015.
18 "The Just-in-Time Professor." House Committee on Education and the Workforce, January 2014.
19 "Not What It Used To Be: American Universities Represent Declining Value for Money to Their Students." *The Economist*, November 29, 2012.
20 "Enrollment in Postsecondary Institutions, Fall 2012; Financial Statistics, Fiscal Year 2012; Graduation Rates, Selected Cohorts, 2004–09; and Employees in Postsecondary Institutions, Fall 2012." Dept. of Education, 2012; Weissmann, Jordan, "Here's Exactly How Much the Government Would Have to Spend to Make Public College Tuition-Free." *The Atlantic*, January 3, 2014.

21 "Federal Higher Education Programs —Overview." The New America Foundation, June 8, 2015.

22 Mitchell, Josh, "White House Floats Bankruptcy Process for Some Student Debt." *Wall Street Journal*, March 10, 2015.

23 "The Low-Wage Recovery and Growing Inequality." National Employment Law Project, August 2012.

24 Casselman, Ben, "Number of the Week: College Grads in Minimum Wage Jobs." *Wall Street Journal*, March 30, 2013.

25 Fry, Richard; Cohn, D'Vera; Livingston, Gretchen; Taylor, Paul: "The Rising Age Gap in Economic Well-Being." Pew Research Center, November 7, 2011.

26 "Why Didn't Higher Education Protect Hispanic and Black Wealth?" St. Louis Federal Reserve, 2015.

27 Jaison R. Abel, Richard Deitz, and Yaqin Su, "Are Recent College Graduates Finding Good Jobs?" New York Federal Reserve, 2014.

28 Matthews, Steve and Smialek, Jeanna, "Pay Penalty Haunts Recession Grads as U.S. Economy Mends." *Bloomberg Business*, July 22, 2014.

29 Harper, Shaun R.; Williams, Collin D.; Blackman, Horatio W.: "Black Male Student-Athletes." Penn GSE, 2013.

30 McCormick, Robert A. and McCormick, Amy Christian, "The Myth of the Student-Athlete: The College Athlete as Employee." Washington Law Review Association, 2006.

31 Strauss, Ben, "N.L.R.B. Rejects Northwestern Football Players' Union Bid." *New York Times*, August 17, 2015.

32 Kram, Jr., Mark, "Review: 'Billion-Dollar Ball' Explores the Economics of College Football's Top Programs." *New York Times*, August 25, 2015.

33 Branch, Taylor, "The Shame of College Sports." *The Atlantic*, October 2011.

34 Wittner, Lawrence, "Why Tuition-Free College Makes Sense." Counterpunch.org, October 28, 2015.

35 Kotch, Alex, "Big Men on Campus: The Koch Brothers' University Donations Are a Veiled Political Weapon." *Salon*, June 19, 2016; "Koch Family Foundations: Koch University Funding—Koch and Academic Freedom." Source Watch, accessed 2016.

36 Fang, Lee, "Koch Responds to Buffett: 'My Business and Non-Profit Investments Are Much More Beneficial to Society.'" Think Progress, August 20, 2011.

37 Buffett, Warren E., "Letter to the Shareholders of Berkshire Hathaway Inc." Berkshire Hathaway, February 27, 2016.

38 Buchheit, Paul, "Candidates for the 2015 'Hypocrite of the Year.'" CommonDreams. org, December 7, 2015.

39 Wilmoth, Daniel, "The Missing Millennial Entrepreneurs." Small Business Administration, February 4, 2016; Cornwall, Jeff, "What Happened to All Those Millennial Entrepreneurs?" Forbes, February 27, 2016.

40 "The Kauffman Index: Startup Activity." The Kauffman Foundation, 2015.

41 Hathaway, Ian and Litan, Robert E., "Declining Business Dynamism in the United States: A Look at States and Metros." Brookings, May 2014; Hamilton, Walter, "A Drop-Off in Start-Ups: Where Are All the Entrepreneurs?" *Los Angeles Times*, September 7, 2014.

42 "Global Entrepreneurs Report 2016." BNP Paribas, November 18, 2015.

43 "Working for the Few." *Oxfam*, January 20, 2014.

44 Johnston, David Cay, "The Great Corporate Cash-Hoarding Crisis." Al Jazeera America, March 14, 2014.

45 Reguly, Eric, "Stock-Based Pay Becomes a Monster as the Rich Get Richer." *The Globe and Mail*, June 25, 2014.

46 Watts, William, "For Every Job Created, Companies Spent $296K on Buybacks." *Market Watch*, November 2, 2015.

47 Worstall, Tim, "Apple Makes $407,000 Profit Per Employee." Forbes, December 28, 2015.

48 "Apple Salaries." Glassdoor, 2016.

49 Barone, Michael, "'Green Jobs' a Dubious Path to the Future." *Washington Examiner*, April 21, 2012.

50 Friedman, Thomas, "Welcome to the Sharing Economy." *New York Times*, July 20, 2013.

51 Worstall, Tim, "Jaron Lanier's 'Who Owns the Future?' What On Earth Is This Guy Talking About? Forbes, May 15, 2013.

52 Stringer, Scott M., "New York City's Millennials in Recession and Recovery." Office of the Comptroller, City of New York, April 2016.

53 Sengupta, Somini, "The World Has a Problem: Too Many Young People." *New York Times*, March 5, 2016.

54 "Guy Ryder announces Global Youth Initiative." International Labour Organization, February 1, 2016.

55 "World Employment and Social Outlook: Trends 2016." International Labour Organization, 2016.

56 Powell, Michael, "The Tragedy of a Hall of Fame Coach and His Star Recruit." *New York Times*, March 4, 2016.

57 "The Most Depressing Student Loan Stories." *Daily Finance*; "9 Students Reveal Their Unbelievable Loan Horror Stories." *Business Insider*; Woodruff, Mandi, "This Bright-Eyed Young Man Was Utterly Demolished by Student Loans." *Business Insider*, May 30, 2012; "Chime in on Private Student Loans." Consumer Financial Protection Bureau, November 16, 2011; Lorin, Janet, "Who's Profiting from $1.2 Trillion of Federal Student Loans?" Bloomberg Business, December 11, 2015; "The Student Loan Documentary." YouTube Video (www.youtube.com/watch?v=wvQR93 C6n2E), accessed May 1, 2016.

## Bibliography

Ginsberg, Benjamin, *The Fall of the Faculty*. Oxford University Press, 2011.

Giroux, Henry A., *Youth in a Suspect Society: Democracy or Disposability?* Palgrave Macmillan, 2009.

# 11

# GUARANTEED JOBS

Some analysts wonder why people in job-deprived areas, like New Orleans after Hurricane Katrina,[1] don't just move to a more work-friendly location.[2] The disposable family,[3] as the thinking implies, would be expected to uproot parents and children, leave behind relatives, friends and neighbors, and restart life in an unfamiliar community with new schools and churches, all in pursuit of a livelihood that has yet to be established.

A guaranteed income will encourage recipients to find local employment, especially if a national commitment were to be made to infrastructure repair,[4] which could create labor-intensive jobs suitable for former manufacturing workers, with minimal additional training. Working-age men and women want jobs rather than handouts. Within long-neglected communities, these jobs should come to willing workers, not the other way around.

Jobs will also be waiting in long-neglected fields like social services. As always, some jobs will pay more than others, but always with the guaranteed minimum. The work chosen by recipients may be entrepreneurial, as newfound incomes unleash talents that were previously suppressed by personal financial concerns, and it could potentially take highly creative forms, as in the 1930s, when the Works Progress Administration hired thousands of artists, actors and musicians to help sustain the cultural needs of the nation. A recent Gallup poll found that nearly 70 percent of workers don't feel "engaged" (enthusiastic and committed) in their jobs.[5] A guaranteed income will help provide the freedom to choose appealing work.

A guaranteed income could also provide **meaningful work in clean energy production**. A study at the University of Massachusetts[6] concluded that at least 1.7 million jobs could be generated by a commitment to wind- and solar-powered renewable energy, about three times as many as in the fossil fuel industry. Half of them would be labor-intensive jobs requiring at most a high school education.

Many of them could help fulfill the futuristic-sounding but inevitable need for solar roads.[7] The prospects grow more enticing each year as recent studies have confirmed the *fast-declining cost of clean energy generation*.[8]

Perhaps most significantly, a guaranteed income could relieve some of the pressure on our newest generation of young adults, who are deep in debt, underemployed, increasingly unable to live on their own, and ill-positioned to take the entrepreneurial chances that are needed to spur innovative business growth. No other group of Americans could make more productive use of an immediate boost in income.

## Notes

1 Gladwell, Malcolm, "Starting Over: Many Katrina Victims Left New Orleans for Good. What Can We Learn from Them?" *The New Yorker*, August 24, 2015.

2 Williamson, Kevin D., "Chaos in the Family, Chaos in the State: The White Working Class's Dysfunction." *National Review*, March 28, 2016.

3 Giroux, Henry, "Dark Waters: Hurricane Katrina, the Politics of Disposability and the Racism of Malcolm Gladwell." Counterpunch.org, September 8, 2015.

4 "Failure to Act: Infrastructure Report Card." American Society of Civil Engineers, 2016.

5 Adkins, Amy, "Majority of U.S. Employees Not Engaged Despite Gains in 2014." Gallup, January 28, 2015.

6 Pollin, Robert; Heintz, James; Garrett-Peltier, Heidi: "The Economic Benefits of Investing in Clean Energy." Center for American Progress, June 2009.

7 "Solar FREAKIN' Roadways!" Solar Roadways (www.youtube.com/watch?v= qlTA3rnpgzU), accessed April 1, 2016.

8 "Levelized Cost of Energy Analysis." Lazard, November 2015.

# 12
## WOMEN

### The Past: A War for Gender Equality

In the early twentieth century, women were fighting for control of their bodies and for the preservation of their families.

#### Abuse vs. Equality[1]

In 1908, a laundry owner by the name of Carl Muller, who was accused of overworking his female employees, took the freedom of contract argument all the way to the Supreme Court. The Court ruled that the protection of women for procreation took priority over their right to free contracts:

> That woman's physical structure and the performance of maternal functions place her at a disadvantage in the struggle for subsistence is obvious...Still again, history discloses the fact that woman has always been dependent upon man...It is impossible to close one's eyes to the fact that she still looks to her brother and depends upon him.

The growing women's movement in the United States was now split between those wishing to protect women in the workplace and those who were advocates for sexual equality.

#### Control of a Woman's Body[2]

On February 11, 1916 women's rights activist Emma Goldman was arrested in New York City for promoting birth control. As a nurse and midwife, she was a fierce advocate for women and children, and a mentor to Planned Parenthood

**FIGURE 12.1** Emma Goldman addressing a crowd at Union Square, New York, 1916.
Corbis Images for Education (https://commons.wikimedia.org/wiki/File:Emma_Goldman_surrounded_by_crowd.jpg).

founder Margaret Sanger. Goldman was nicknamed "Red Emma"—partly because of her socialist views, partly because of her Russian heritage. Her like-minded husband, Alexander Berkman, who was also Russian, had been imprisoned for attempting to kill Henry Frick, the owner of Carnegie Steel, during a violent workers' strike.

Emma Goldman and her husband ended their stay in the U.S. in a predictable manner, protesting America's entry into World War I and the accompanying draft. They spent two years in prison and then were deported. When she died, she was buried in Chicago's Waldheim Cemetery, the burial place of the anarchists who were hanged for their role in the Haymarket Riots.

On October 26, 1916 Margaret Sanger was arrested in Brooklyn, New York for running a birth control clinic. She had opened the clinic on October 16, but the authorities didn't quite know what was going on, and needed ten days to find an 1873 law that considered any discussion of reproduction obscene. They managed to drum up a charge of "public nuisance."

Sanger was a strong advocate for women's rights, a socialist, a union activist, author of the feminist magazine *The Woman Rebel*, and notorious for affairs with several men, including author H.G. Wells. In 1914, in order to avoid prosecution on a number of sex charges, she fled to Europe, where a more sexually liberated climate allowed her to better learn her craft. She returned to the U.S. in 1915 with considerable popular support, which helped to get the still-pending charges dropped. She began preparing for her birth control clinic. But puritanical opponents stood in her way.

At Sanger's trial after her October 26, 1916 arrest, the trial judge summarized his opposition to birth control by declaring that women did not have "the right to copulate with a feeling of security that there will be no resulting conception." The accused spent 30 days in jail. But the stiff resistance to women's rights just made her stronger. Her outspoken battle against "back-alley" abortions endeared her to the female public. In 1921, she founded the American Birth Control League, which eventually became Planned Parenthood. She opened an all-female clinic in New York City, and an all-black clinic in Harlem, all the while lobbying tirelessly for federal support, which wouldn't come until 1938, when the federal ban on birth control was lifted—although it took until 1965 for full legalization.

Margaret Sanger arrived at a time when women had almost no information on childbirth, miscarriage, birth control, and abortion, largely because a conservative and male-dominated Congress had long considered the vital information obscene. Sanger vowed to help every woman become "the absolute mistress of her own body."

### *Drunken Husbands*[3]

**FIGURE 12.2** Crowded bar at midnight, June 30, 1919, just before prohibition went into effect.
Library of Congress (http://www.loc.gov/pictures/item/99405168/).

**FIGURE 12.3** Agents pour liquor into New York sewer following a raid.
Library of Congress (www.loc.gov/pictures/item/99405169/).

On October 28, 1919 Congress passed the Volstead Act, leading to the 18th Amendment and Prohibition in America. Thanks to decades of advocacy by suffragists and temperance supporters Elizabeth Cady Stanton, Susan B. Anthony, Frances Willard, and Carrie Nation, the country finally recognized the debilitating effects of alcohol, especially on the family men who would fritter away their earnings on whiskey and then take out their dark frustrations on defenseless wives.

America has always been a hard-drinking nation. George Washington kept his troops happy with rum and whiskey; John Adams started every day with hard cider; Abraham Lincoln sold barrels of whiskey at his grocery store in New Salem, IL. Early Americans drank at every meal, including breakfast. Church bells rang twice a day to signal "grog time." Physicians recommended whiskey and beer over water hauled from rivers and ponds. By 1830, the average American over 15 drank 88 bottles of whiskey every year, three times as much as today.

In the early 1900s, the Anti-Saloon League became as powerful a lobbying organization as the NRA a hundred years later. By shrewdly associating beer with our World War I German enemies, the 18th Amendment was all but finalized.

But Prohibition flopped. The restaurant industry fell off dramatically without their alcohol concessions. Jobs were lost as waiters and truckers and bottlers had no one to hire them, and as a result the federal government lost billions of dollars in tax revenue. Yet loopholes to the new law were proliferating. Since pharmacists could prescribe whiskey for illness, bootleggers opened their own pharmacies. New churches providentially opened, taking advantage of the religious wine exemption. And home brewing turned millions of Americans into criminals. So many cases came to court, and so trivial the charges, that the judicial system began to fall apart.

Still, women's voices had been heard.

## The Present: Women Still Beaten Down[4]

In 1955, Mrs. Dale Carnegie, whose husband wrote the best-seller *How to Win Friends and Influence People*, advised her fellow housewives:

> The two big steps that women must take are to help their husbands decide where they are going and use their pretty heads to help them get there. Let's face it, girls. That wonderful guy in your house—and in mine—is building your house, your happiness and the opportunities that will come to your children.[5]

Women were second-rate members of society and marriage in the 1950s.[6] Those who went out to work were relegated to low-paying clerical, nursing, teaching, and domestic jobs, and to even lower-paying jobs for the nearly invisible black female population. The newspaper want-ads had a separate section for women. The same type of humiliation existed in higher education, where many medical schools, law schools, and graduate schools were rejecting the "frivolous" applications of women, while female undergraduate students were often said to be pursuing an M.R.S. (Mrs.) degree.

The women's rights movement of the 60s and 70s contributed to some dramatic changes in education. Based on data from the Census Bureau and the Russell Sage Foundation:[7]

- By 2009, women were earning 33 percent *more undergraduate degrees than men*.
- In 1970, about 50 percent more men than women completed master's degrees. By 2010, about 50 percent *more women than men completed master's degrees*.
- In 1970, women earned about 10 percent of all PhDs. Now they earn *more PhDs than men*.[8]

The greatest degree of growth, for all levels of higher education, has occurred within the black and Hispanic female communities.[9] But despite all the successes of women, and despite their having earned the right to economic equality, the white male establishment has prevailed, like a schoolyard bully muscling lunch money from the smarter but weaker kids. Only one out of five members of Congress is female. Corporate boards remain overwhelmingly male.[10]

The disparagement of women goes well beyond the levels of higher education:

## Income: $1 for a Woman, $1.25 for a Man

The Bureau of Labor Statistics reports that women earn just 80 percent of men's pay.[11] Income disparities[12] have worsened since the recession, with only about one-fifth of new jobs going to women. In California, Hispanic women, who do much of our homecare work, make only 43 cents for every dollar made by white men.[13]

## Retirement Wealth: $1 for a Woman, $1.80 for a Man

Men average nearly $28,000 a year in retirement assets, while women have just over $15,000.[14] Women over 65 have twice the poverty rate of men. Unsurprisingly, black and Hispanic women fare the worst, with median wealth of a stunningly low $200 and $100, respectively.[15]

## Women's Health: Congress Cares More About Controlling the Female Body

Income disparities threaten the health of women, especially low-income black women, who are three to four times as likely to die from pregnancy issues as white women.[16] A recent scientific study[17] found that the gender wage gap causes significantly more anxiety and depression in women. It gets worse with attacks on Planned Parenthood, which saves women's lives through breast cancer screenings, and reduces abortions by providing contraceptive services, all while saving an estimated $7 in health costs for every dollar spent.[18]

The safety net, with programs geared toward children's nutrition and infant care, is repeatedly under attack, even though the total cost of assistance is much less than welfare for the rich.[19]

## Women Are Respected—In Other Countries

The U.S. has one of the fastest-increasing rates of maternal mortality in the world, putting us in the company of war-torn and impoverished nations.[20] The U.S., Oman, and Papua New Guinea are the only countries that don't provide paid maternity leave.[21]

Our country ranks #8 on the UN's 2015 Human Development Index, but when adjusted for *gender inequality* it *drops to #55*.[22]

Just about 100 years ago, Margaret Sanger, the founder of Planned Parenthood and a tireless advocate for a woman's right to control her own body, spoke about the poor urban women of New York City: "These poor, pale-faced, wretched wives. The men beat them. They cringe before their blows, but pick up the baby, dirty and unkempt, and return to serve him."[23]

Women are still getting beaten down today.

## Personal Stories of Women in America[24]

### *Today's Margaret Sanger*

*The Atlantic* published stories of women who dealt with the personal anguish of terminating a pregnancy. A 15-year-old girl in California was impregnated by a 39-year-old man, and afterwards she found herself living on the street, without a job, taking drugs when she could get them. She knew she was incapable of raising a child.

Planned Parenthood explained the options available to her. She chose abortion. In her own words, "I had been manipulated by a pedophile, but thankfully I was not forced to have his child."

A Texas woman learned that the fetus she was carrying had a brain abnormality, "100 percent incompatible with life." Planned Parenthood explained that because of state law, she would have to endure a four-day process of counseling, mandatory waiting, and dilation of the cervix before receiving treatment. She was fortunate enough to have the money to fly to an out-of-state abortion provider, where the procedure was done in one day. Sadly, few women seeking such assistance have that option.

### *Strong Women, Embattled Women*

Candidates for "Most Remarkable Person" must include Doretha Ford, an 84-year-old woman in the Austin area of Chicago's west side. Doretha spent her childhood in the fields of Mississippi, picking cotton for her sharecropper family, often working from dawn to dusk, filling bags with 60 pounds of cotton, repeating the drudgery day after day until she finally had the chance as a young wife and mother to move to Chicago in 1952. Doretha had ten children, three of whom are severely mentally disabled. For over 50 years, she has cared for her three homebound children, feeding and bathing them, changing their diapers, spending many hours patiently sitting with them in her sparsely furnished but comfortable living room.

As we sat together talking, Doretha gently tended to her 52-year-old daughter, who made incomprehensible sounds as her arms repeatedly lurched up and down, and then side to side, as if she were trying to express herself in my presence. It quickly became apparent that Doretha had readily accepted her role in life, even embraced it. She seemed contented amidst the family members who depended on her. She spoke of the worst mornings, when her body ached, but she knew

**FIGURE 12.4** Doretha, Chicago, IL.
Personal photo taken by author on February 12, 2016.

she couldn't stay in bed; she often cried in those early dawn hours. Her only private moments came after her children went to bed at 9 p.m., when she could read, watch TV, or just enjoy the silence. But she was happy. She spoke of her faith in God, the spiritual strength that had sustained her for 75 years, from the sweltering cotton fields of Mississippi to the frigid streets of Chicago. "I'm blessed," she said with a smile. She eagerly agreed to have her picture taken, although she insisted that I give her a minute to change her sweater and fix her hair.

Brenda (a pseudonym) was a 35-year-old student in a writing class at Chicago's St. Leonard's Ministry, a center for education and job placement for formerly incarcerated men and women. Brenda was a model student, reliable and hard-working and proficient at writing. She spoke very little, but her input was welcome, her too-infrequent smile infectious.

But Brenda was a felon. She had been caught shoplifting 15 years earlier. As a young single mother, she had stolen food from Wal-Mart, partly because she was embarrassed by her dependency on her mother, but mostly, as she admitted in one of her essays, because she was not a very good person in her younger days. Her recklessness made it hard for her to find a job, and even to find a place to live. A GED from St. Leonard's helped her gain a position in a culinary school.

Her two daughters were older now, able to assist with the chores after school, and freeing their mother, finally, to seek a career and a degree of independence for her family.

> I've had a very troubled life.
>
> Nickole, a resident at Grace House in Chicago

At the age of nine, her two step-sisters and their boyfriends took her along to kidnap a man who owed them money from a drug deal. After tying him up and beginning to ransack his house, looking for valuables, they told Nickole to deal with the man's barking dog, but she couldn't get it to quiet down. She kicked the dog and kept kicking it until she killed it.

Nickole went to the Audi Home for six months, where she was physically abused by the older girls. When other kids were starting high school she was a rebel. She learned about drugs. Throughout her teen years she took cocaine, eventually moving to heroin, supporting her worsening habit by shoplifting, and by the age of 17 being charged as an adult for theft. In and out of Cook County jail, life continued to spiral downward. Nickole sold her body for drug money. She was impregnated by a man who then took up with a 15-year-old in the next door apartment. At the age of 21, she found another man, by whom she had her second child, a boy, but a few weeks later the new father took out his gun and shot himself in the head.

Nickole has tried to understand why she went bad. Her domineering mother came from a strict white family that was troubled by alcoholism. Her father is black, and, as she remembers, a heavy cocaine user. Divorce for the two of them came when Nickole was four years old. "I was angry at my mother for being white because I felt she was to blame why I didn't have any friends…I abused her."

In the 1990s, even with two small children, drugs remained the center of Nickole's existence. "Withdrawal is horrible. You're sick, you're throwing up, you're shitting on yourself…I just knew I had to do what I had to do to get one more…I slashed the face of a drug store manager…I slept in abandoned buildings, I slept in storage bins, I slept under porches." She slept with anyone willing to give her money. She was under court-ordered house arrest for much of her young adult life, but she snuck out at night, turned tricks with regular customers in the alley behind her sister's house, kept snorting heroin, spent more months in jail, and then finally got the opportunity in early 2015 to enter Grace House, the women's division of Chicago's St. Leonard's Rehab Center.

While Nickole was finally, at the age of 43, getting her life in order, her 25-year-old daughter Che'von died of a drug overdose.

> I sold my children. Not literally, but I neglected them, I missed a big chunk of both their lives.

But Grace House has made a difference. Nickole has been addiction-free, with no desire to return to the dark days behind her. She plans to get a job when rehab is done, to support herself, to live independently and responsibly for the first time in her life. And she's succeeding. Hollie, the director of Grace House, calls Nickole "an inspiration" to the other women at the center.

Desiree Metcalf, 24, lives in a rural New York town with three daughters, six, four, and two. As a young girl she suffered from mental problems, and then alcoholism, and she tried to kill herself. Now her six-year-old is showing the same signs of instability, attempting to run away from home in the middle of the night.
    Desiree isn't lazy. She trained to become a certified nursing assistant, but can't find a job, and her employment prospects disappeared when someone totaled her car. Mass transit is virtually nonexistent in her rural area. But even if she were to get a job, the increased income would make her ineligible for government programs, most importantly childcare. Already, her family's food stamp benefits had been cut from $700 to $200 because her husband starting working part-time at McDonald's. But after getting the job, he left the family. Desiree has other issues: gum disease has taken her top row of teeth, and even though she's eligible for Medicaid, local clinics refuse to accept it.

Sister Rita is Director of Senior Services at Marillac House. Her summer cooling program includes about 100 elderly women, most in their 80s and 90s, many still living in the proud old buildings of their impoverished but dignified East Austin community in Chicago. Rita recalled visiting Naomi, a fiercely independent 90-year-old blind woman who lives alone. She couldn't really take care of herself anymore. Roaches scurried about in the kitchen, the stench of urine permeated the whole area. Now it was even worse, because Illinois' new governor had cut the funding for the cooling program. When Naomi didn't respond to Senior Services one day, the fire department paramedics were called, and she was found unconscious in her unbearably hot living room. Today, Sister Rita added encouragingly, the elderly woman is safely housed at a nursing facility.
    Sister Rita spoke of the lady with the walker who made her way eight blocks once a week to stand in line for the food pantry. She mentioned the hoarders, who go years unwilling to throw out anything of even minor value. She laughed about the "ice cream lady" who wouldn't let any Marillac workers in her house until they showed up one day with ice cream.
    As difficult as life can be for the inner-city elderly women, they are generally happy people, according to Sister Rita. They don't expect much from life; they remain contented with the little pleasures brought to them by friends and family. "I'm blessed" is a common refrain when the Marillac reps inquire about their lives.

# Notes

1 "Women Working, 1800–1930." *Harvard University Library Open Collections Program*.
2 "Birth Control Pioneer Arrested." *This Day in History* (February 11, 1916), History. com; "Margaret Sanger." *United States History*, u-s-history.com.
3 Burns, Ken, *Prohibition*. Public Broadcasting System; "The Temperance Movement." *United States History*, u-s-history.com.
4 Buchheit, Paul, "The Many Ways Women Are Beaten Down in America." NationOfChange.org, October 5, 2015.
5 *Better Homes and Gardens*, April, 1955.
6 Buchheit, Paul, *Boomer Boys*. CreateSpace, 2010.
7 "The Rise of Women: Seven Charts Showing Women's Rapid Gains in Educational Achievement." Russell Sage Foundation, February 21, 2013; Jeffrey, Terence P., "25% Fewer Men Than Women Graduate College." CNS News, June 24, 2012.
8 Women earned just over 50% of doctoral degrees in 2009–10 (op. cit. Russell Sage Foundation).
9 "Fast Facts: Degrees conferred by sex and race." National Center for Education Statistics, 2012.
10 "Tracking Gender Diversity on Corporate Boards." Thomson Reuters, October 22, 2014.
11 "20 Facts About U.S. Inequality that Everyone Should Know." The Stanford Center on Poverty and Inequality.
12 Showalter, Amelia and Wilson, Chris, "How the Pay Gap Hurts Women's Financial Security." *Time*, March 3, 2016.
13 Adams, Susan, "Are Women Catching Up in Pay?" Forbes, April 9, 2013.
14 Edwards, Haley Sweetland, "Inside the Next Social Security Crisis." *Time*, July 23, 2015.
15 Chang, Mariko, "Women & Wealth: Insights for Grantmakers." *Asset Funders Network*, 2015.
16 "Deadly Delivery." *Amnesty International*, Spring 2011.
17 Platt, Jonathan; Prins, Seth; Bates, Lisa; Keyes, Katherine: "Unequal Depression for Equal Work?" *Social Science & Medicine*, January 2016.
18 "Breast Cancer Screenings." Planned Parenthood (www.plannedparenthood.org/ learn/womens-health/breast-cancer-screenings), accessed August 15, 2015; Frost, Jennifer J.; Sonfield, Adam; Zolna, Mia R.; Finer, Lawrence B., "Return on Investment: A Fuller Assessment of the Benefits and Cost Savings of the US Publicly Funded Family Planning Program." *The Milbank Quarterly*, Vol. 92, No. 4, 2014.
19 Buchheit, Paul, "Some Numbers for the 'Entitlement' Bashers." NationOfChange. org, August 25, 2014.
20 "Global, Regional, and National Levels and Causes of Maternal Mortality During 1990–2013." *The Lancet*, September 2014.
21 Talbot, Margaret, "America's Family-Leave Disgrace." *The New Yorker*, January 22, 2015.
22 "Human Development Report 2015." United Nations Development Programme, 2015.
23 Chesler, Ellen, *Woman of Valor: Margaret Sanger and the Birth Control Movement in America*. Simon & Schuster, 1992.

24 Bodenner, Chris, "Personal Stories of Abortion Made Public." *The Atlantic*, March 3, 2016; Personal Interviews: Doretha, Brenda, Nickole; Fessler, Pam, "One Family's Story Shows How the Cycle of Poverty Is Hard to Break." NPR, June 10, 2014; Personal Interview: Sister Rita, Marillac House, Chicago, December 2015.

## Bibliography

Chesler, Ellen, *Woman of Valor: Margaret Sanger and the Birth Control Movement in America.* Simon & Schuster, 1992.

Downey, Kirstin, *The Woman Behind the New Deal*. Anchor, 2010.

Shiva, Vandana, *Staying Alive: Women, Ecology, and Development*. North Atlantic Books, 2016.

# 13

# A TALE OF EXTREMES

The wealthy working people have earned their right to live in the city. They went out, got an education, work hard, and earned it. I shouldn't have to worry about being accosted. I shouldn't have to see the pain, struggle, and despair of homeless people to and from my way to work every day.

Justin Keller, San Francisco tech entrepreneur[1]

Beverly is a middle-aged homeless woman who survives day-by-day on the streets of Chicago. Joseph, an advocate for the homeless and a volunteer at a community kitchen on the city's north side, noticed Beverly huddled in a theater exitway on a frigid November morning, cup in hand, a pair of crutches leaning against the door behind her. He gave her a little money, and she responded with a smile and a subdued "thank you." They talked a little bit; she seemed eager to share a few minutes of conversation. She mentioned that she hadn't eaten that day. Since they were too far from the community kitchen, Joe offered to buy her a meal. Her favorite was chili, at a lunch spot around the corner.[2]

Charles and David Koch are both members of the 0.00001 percent. That's a group of twenty individuals who have a total net worth of over a half-trillion dollars, an average of $26 billion each. One of David's residences is at 740 Park Avenue, in the most exclusive area of Manhattan. The doorman at the 740 building had this to say about David Koch: "We would load up his trucks—two vans, usually—every weekend, for the Hamptons...multiple guys, in and out, in and out, heavy bags. We would never get a tip from Mr. Koch. We would never get a smile from Mr. Koch. Fifty-dollar check for Christmas."[3]

## Comforts

Beverly had made $8 that day, from 8 a.m. to 2 p.m., a little over a dollar an hour. She needed $22 for a night in a Single Room Occupancy (SRO) hotel, where she could shower and have some privacy, and most importantly feel safe for a few hours. The alternative was a local mission, where, she said, "You got to sleep with your stuff under you, so that nobody will steal it from you." She also spoke reluctantly about the bedbugs.

Hamptons home builder Joe Farrell described some of the extravagances of his creations: a home ATM machine "regularly restocked with $20,000 in $10 bills" and a store selling $30,000 bottles of Dom Perignon.[4] A trifle for someone like David Koch, who made $3 million an hour from his investments in 2014.

## Perspectives

As Joe walked with her to the restaurant, Beverly told him she felt lucky to be in Chicago, with several nearby Resource Centers where she could apply for food stamps. He remembered pausing for a moment before they went inside, as Beverly, balancing nimbly on her crutches, deposited her empty paper cup in a trash bin. If she is approved for food stamps, she'll get about $1.50 per meal.

Between the time Charles and David Koch went to bed and woke up on any given night in 2014, they would have accumulated enough stock market wealth to get a room for the night for every one of the *633 thousand homeless Americans*.

Charles Koch said, "I want my fair share and that's all of it."[5]

## Extreme Inequality Is Getting Even More Extreme

The 20 richest Americans now own more wealth than the bottom half of the U.S. population.[6] As of 2014, our country had the fourth-highest degree of wealth inequality in the world, trailing only Russia, Ukraine, and Lebanon.[7] American individuals or families, including Bill Gates, the Koch brothers and the Walton siblings, *each own* approximately *one-thousandth* of our nation's $86 trillion in total wealth.[8]

As inequality grows, America's infrastructure is falling into a state of dangerous disrepair.[9] Attempts to save money by changing the water source for Flint, Michigan resulted in the lead poisoning of thousands of children, and the Centers for Disease Control estimates that over a half-million children nationwide are suffering from some degree of lead poisoning.[10] Yet in 2012, Congress cut the funding for lead programs by nearly half.[11]

Instead of paying taxes to help address our infrastructure problems, the wealthiest Americans have formed, according to the *New York Times*, an "income defense industry" to shelter their riches, with "a high-priced phalanx of lawyers, estate planners, lobbyists and anti-tax activists who exploit and defend a dizzying array of tax maneuvers, virtually none of them available to taxpayers of more modest means."[12]

Extreme inequality, and the tax avoidance that contributes to it, is even worse on a global scale.[13] According to Oxfam, just 62 of the world's richest individuals now own as much wealth as the poorest half of the world, about 3.6 billion people.[14] The recently published *Panama Papers* reveal that greed and tax cheating are indeed universal phenomena.[15]

## Economic Terrorism[16]

The 0.01 percent consists of sixteen thousand individuals, about the size of a crowd at a professional basketball game. The inequality horror they've fomented is reaching far beyond the half of America that is in or near poverty, for it now impacts those of us well above the median, those of us in the second highest of four wealth quartiles.

### 1. The 0.01 Percent Have as Much Wealth as 80 Percent of America

The combined net worth of the sixteen thousand richest Americans is approximately the same as the total wealth of 256 million people.

### 2. Americans with up to a Quarter-Million Dollars Are Part of a Group with Less Wealth Than the 0.01 Percent

That group encompasses 80 percent of us, and includes even Americans with a net worth up to about $277,000.

### 3. The 0.01 Percent Owns about as Much as 75 Percent of the Entire World

The world's poorest 75 percent own roughly four percent of total global wealth, approximately the same percentage of wealth owned by the 0.01 percent in the United States. A super-rich basketball crowd owns as much wealth as three-quarters of the world.

### 4. The 0.01 Percent—Who Are They?

It starts with the billionaires, the Forbes 400 and 136 more, for a total of 536 individuals with a total net worth of $2.6 trillion at the end of 2015.

It continues with more Ultra High Net Worth Individuals (UHNWIs). These loftily named people, over fifteen thousand of them, are worth hundreds of millions of dollars apiece, bringing the total 0.01 percent wealth to about $6.2 trillion, based on 2013–14 data.[17] But U.S. wealth has grown by about 30 percent in three years, and the Forbes 400 has grown by 38 percent, and thus the *total wealth of the 0.01 percent has grown to over $9 trillion.*

In contrast, a recent Institute for Policy Studies report[18] calculated that the bottom half of America has about $732 billion in total wealth, and further calculations on the same data show that the *bottom 75 percent of America owned about $6.2 trillion* in 2013.

Three-quarters of Americans *together own much less* than that billionaire basketball crowd.

## Notes

1 Wong, Julia Carrie, "San Francisco Tech Worker: 'I Don't Want to See Homeless Riff-Raff.'" *The Guardian*, February 18, 2016.
2 Personal Interview, November 19, 2013.
3 Mayer, Jane, "A Word from Our Sponsor." *The New Yorker*, May 27, 2013.
4 Rutenberg, Jim, "Hamptons McMansions Herald a Return of Excess." *New York Times*, August 26, 2013.
5 Palast, Greg, *The Best Democracy Money Can Buy*. Plume, 2004.
6 Collins, Chuck and Hoxie, Josh, "Billionaire Bonanza." Institute for Policy Studies, December 1, 2015.
7 "Global Wealth Databook 2013." Credit Suisse, October 2013.
8 Forbes 400 (www.forbes.com/forbes-400/), accessed December 21, 2015.
9 "America's Infrastructure Report Card." *American Society of Civil Engineers*, 2013.
10 "Blood Lead Levels in Children Aged 1–5 Years—United States, 1999–2010." Centers for Disease Control and Prevention, April 5, 2013.
11 Kristof, Nicholas, "America Is Flint." *New York Times*, February 7, 2016.
12 Scheiber, Noam and Cohen, Patricia, "For the Wealthiest, a Private Tax System That Saves Them Billions." *New York Times*, December 29, 2015.
13 Personal Analysis, December 1, 2014 (www.usagainstgreed.org/20141201_Analysis. txt), accessed November 15, 2016.
14 "An Economy for the 1%." *Oxfam International*, 2016.
15 MacFarquhar, Neil and Castle, Stephen, "Panama Papers Continue to Shake Leaders, Including Cameron and Putin." *New York Times*, April 7, 2016.
16 Buchheit, Paul, "The Real Terrorists: The .01%." CommonDreams.org, January 11, 2016; Personal Analysis, January 11, 2016 (www.youdeservefacts.org/20160111_ Analysis.txt), accessed November 14, 2016.
17 "American Ultra Wealth Ranking 2014–2015." *Wealth-X*. Wealthx.com.
18 Collins, Chuck and Hoxie, Josh, op. cit.

# 14

## SOLDIERS

**FIGURE 14.1** African-Americans collecting bones of soldiers killed in battle. Cold Harbor, VA., April 1865.

Library of Congress: John Reekie, photographer (http://commons.wikimedia.org/wiki/File:Cold_Harbor,_Va._African_Americans_collecting_bones.jpg).

## The Past: The Horrors of War

> Night brought quiet. But out of that silence rose new sounds, more appalling still…a smothered moan…cries for help, some begging for a drop of water, some calling on God for pity, and some on friendly hands to finish what the enemy had so horribly begun. Some with delirious, dreamy voices murmuring loved names as if the dearest were bending over them.
>
> Fredericksburg, 1863[1]

> That night, brush fires raged through the woods. 200 wounded federal soldiers burned alive, while the entrenched soldiers listened to their screams.
>
> Battle of The Wilderness, 1864

### *Andersonville*[2]

### *The Camp*

With the warm weather the condition of the swamp in the center of the prison became simply horrible…In the slimy ooze were billions of white maggots. They would crawl out by thousands on the warm sand, and, lying there a few minutes, sprout a wing or a pair of them. With these they would essay a clumsy flight, ending by dropping down upon some exposed portion of a man's body, and stinging him like a gad-fly. Still worse, they would drop into what he was cooking, and the utmost care could not prevent a mess of food from being contaminated with them…Every scouped out pea (or bean) which found its way into the soup bore inside of its shell from ten to twenty of these hard-crusted little weevils.

The sinks over the lower portions of the stream were imperfect in their plan and structure, and the excrements were in large measure deposited so near the borders of the stream as not to be washed away, or else accumulated upon the low boggy ground. The volume of water was not sufficient to wash away the feces, and they accumulated in such quantities in the lower portion of the stream as to form a mass of liquid excrement…Millions of flies swarmed over everything, and covered the faces of the sleeping patients, and crawled down their open mouths, and deposited their maggots in the gangrenous wounds of the living, and in the mouths of the dead… The groans of the thousands of sick around us, the shrieks of the rotting ones in the gangrene wards rang incessantly in our ears.

**FIGURE 14.2** Andersonville Prison, Ga., August 17, 1864. View of stockade showing the dead-line.

Library of Congress: Civil War Photograph Collection (https://commons.wikimedia.org/wiki/File:Andersonville_pow_tents_photo.jpg).

**FIGURE 14.3** Drawing rations; view from main gate. Andersonville Prison, Georgia, August 17, 1864.

Federal Works Agency, National Archives (https://commons.wikimedia.org/wiki/File:Drawing_rations,_view_from_main_gate._Andersonville_Prison,_Georgia,_August_17,_1864.,_08-17-1964_-_NARA_-_533034.tif).

## Sickness

[Scurvy] usually manifested itself first in the mouth. The breath became unbearably fetid; the gums swelled until they protruded, livid and disgusting, beyond the lips. The teeth became so loose that they frequently fell out, and the sufferer would pick them up and set them back in their sockets. In attempting to bite the hard corn bread furnished by the bakery the teeth often stuck fast and were pulled out. The gums had a fashion of breaking away, in large chunks, which would be swallowed or spit out. All the time one was eating his mouth would be filled with blood, fragments of gums and loosened teeth.

Frightful, malignant ulcers appeared in other parts of the body; the ever-present maggot flies laid eggs in these, and soon worms swarmed therein. The sufferer looked and felt as if, though he yet lived and moved, his body was anticipating the rotting it would undergo a little later in the grave.

To my right was a handsome young Sergeant of an Illinois Infantry Regiment, captured at Kenesaw. His left arm had been amputated between the shoulder and elbow, and he was turned into the Stockade with the stump all undressed, save the ligating of the arteries. Of course, he had not been inside an hour until the maggot flies had laid eggs in the open wound, and before the day was gone the worms were hatched out, and rioting amid the inflamed and super-sensitive nerves, where their every motion was agony…I do not think he ate or slept for a week before he died.

**FIGURE 14.4** How they buried them. Andersonville Prison, Georgia, August 17, 1864.
Federal Works Agency, National Archives (https://commons.wikimedia.org/wiki/File:How_they_buried_them._Andersonville_Prison,_Georgia,_August_17,_1864.,_08-17-1864_-_NARA_-_533035.tif).

## Death

Home-loving, kindly-hearted men, especially those who had passed out of the first flush of youth, and had left wife and children behind when they entered the service, were speedily overcome with despair of surviving until released; their hopelessness fed on the same germs which gave it birth, until it became senseless, vacant-eyed, unreasoning, incurable melancholy, when the victim would lie for hours, without speaking a word, except to babble of home, or would wander aimlessly about the camp—frequently stark naked—until he died or was shot for coming too near the Dead Line.

## Letters to Loved Ones[3]

**Civil War**: On the evening of May 10, 1864, 26-year-old Confederate Private James Robert Montgomery wrote to his father in Camden, Mississippi, dripping blood on the letter as he formed his final words:

Dear Father. This is my last letter to you. I have been struck by a piece of shell and my right shoulder is horribly mangled and I know death is inevitable...I know death is near, that I will die far from home...Give my love to all my friends. My strength fails me...Again, a long farewell to you. May we meet in heaven.

The family was never able to find their son's grave.

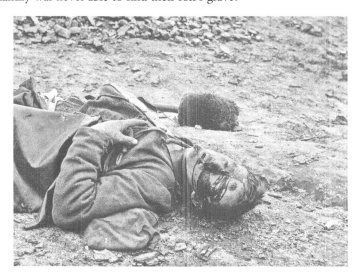

**FIGURE 14.5** Dead South Carolina soldier in trench, Petersburg, Va., April 1865.
Library of Congress: Author Thomas C Roche (https://commons.wikimedia.org/wiki/File:Dead_soldier_(American_Civil_War_-_Siege_of_Petersburg,_April_1_1865)_(2).jpg).

**Civil War**: Capt. David Embree writes to his sister Rose, February 3, 1863:

Dear Sister, The bullet came obliquely from the left and front and passed several feet in front of me. It seemed that I could almost hear it singing from the time it left its bed in the rebel's gun. Suddenly I heard the same ball go crash! and I knew by the sound that it had burst a human skull...We could not refrain from casting a glance at the man who lay there trembling in every limb and the blood spirting from his nostrils...

**World War I**: 'Dickwitch' writes to his friend Elmer J. Sutters:

Dear Old Bunkie, It was here, old man, that I got my first Hun with the bayonet. We were pressing through a thicket when this big plug-ugly Hun suddenly loomed up in front of me. It was my first hand to hand fight. I parried off his blow and had him through his throat. He went down like a log...He never even made a sound.

**World War II**: Pvt. Morton D. Elevitch writes to his mother from Fort Benning, Georgia, November 23, 1943:

This week they're teaching us to kill...They teach us how to withdraw our bayonets in a certain manner, because steel sticks to warm human flesh.

**World War II**: New Yorker Rupert Trimmingham, April 28, 1944:

Myself and eight other Negro soldiers...We could not purchase a cup of coffee at any of the lunchrooms...About two dozen German prisoners of war...entered the lunchroom, sat at the tables, had their meals served, talked, smoked...I stood on the outside looking on.

**Vietnam War**: Private Timothy G. Robinson of Hoyt Lakes, Minnesota, April 14, 1968:

I hope God will bring me back home so that I may marry the girl I love, which will be in March if things go OK.

Robinson stepped on a landmine five days later and was killed instantly.

**The end of the Vietnam War** brought reflection on the damage done, the devastation of life and livelihood, the disdain by American soldiers for a people considered inferior even in their own country. Said radio operator Fred Widmer, "Your attitude towards the villagers, now—everybody's an enemy...Instead of just going through villages, casually going through them, you went into villages, started ripping shit apart." Added squad leader Lawrence La Croix, "We were to

**FIGURE 14.6** Aftermath of the My Lai massacre, March 16, 1968.
Photographer Ronald L. Haeberle (https://commons.wikimedia.org/wiki/File:My_Lai_massacre.jpg).

**FIGURE 14.7** Woman killed by US soldiers. Part of her brain is lying nearby.
Photographer Ronald L. Haeberle (https://commons.wikimedia.org/wiki/File:Dead_woman_from_the_My_Lai_massacre.jpg).

shoot literally anything that moved. If it was growing, cut it down. If it was a building, burn it. If it was a well, poison it. If it was alive, kill it."

In My Lai,[4] the soldiers gathered together about 170 old men and women, and mothers with small children. Truong Tham, a My Lai villager, recalled: "They start to take us all away. Everyone in the house, they took us to leave, all of us were taken away." Added another villager, Pham Thi Tuan: "I held one of my children, and led the other one. I walked with them until they told us to stop. They made us walk from inside the village, across the rice fields. I pulled my kids to go with me. I dragged my kids, but they still hit us, kicked us."

Rifleman James Dursi testified at Calley's trial: "Lieutenant Calley and a weeping rifleman named Paul D. Meadlo—the same soldier who had fed candy to the children before shooting them—pushed the prisoners into the ditch... There was an order to shoot by Lieutenant Calley...I was crying...Calley and Meadlo pointed their rifles into the ditch and fired...People were diving on top of each other; mothers were trying to protect their children."

It was mostly women, children and old men, bayoneted and tortured and raped before being dragged screaming to the ditch. One soldier admitted, "I cut their throats, cut off their hands, cut out their tongues, scalped them. I did it. A lot of people were doing it and I just followed."

Throughout the duration of the war, some seven million tons of bombs had been dropped on Vietnam, more than twice the tonnage of World War II, and equivalent to a 500-pound bomb for every human being in Vietnam. Many of the survivors were burned by napalm—jellied gasoline. One woman, according to a 1965 *New York Times* dispatch repeated by Howard Zinn, had "both arms burned off by napalm and her eyelids so badly burned that she cannot close them. When it is time for her to sleep her family puts a blanket over her head." Among the innocents, the level of despair matched the physical pain.

## The Present: Disposable Victims of War[5]

> They are not very good at feeding their people, but they invest a huge amount in their weapons.
>> President Barack Obama. He was talking about North Korea.

In the U.S., where half the discretionary budget is spent on the military, one out of five children live in food insecure households.[6]

The U.S. currently has its special forces in 147 countries—75 percent of the nations on the planet. That includes Green Berets, Navy SEALs, Air Force Commandos, Army Rangers, Marine Corps Raiders, and a slew of analysts, planners, and administrative personnel.[7]

Since 9/11, we have contributed to the breakdown of societies in Iraq, Afghanistan, Syria, and Libya while fomenting resentment and blowback among their terrorized citizens. Two days after President Obama expressed grief and anger about the Oregon school shootings, a hospital in Afghanistan was bombed by the U.S., killing 22 people. Our government admitted its mistake. But we haven't apologized for funding Saudi Arabia's attacks in Yemen, which are killing hundreds of civilians. Or for our drone strikes in Pakistan, where even by the most conservative estimates[8] hundreds of families have faced death by drones, causing one 13-year-old Pakistani boy to say, "I no longer love blue skies...The drones do not fly when the skies are gray."

The U.S. is using *algorithms* to kill. Computer calculations determine the location of enemy targets, and then lists are compiled to schedule their killings. The whistleblower for "The Drone Papers"[9] spoke of "This outrageous explosion...of monitoring people and racking and stacking them on lists, assigning them numbers, assigning them 'baseball cards,' assigning them death sentences without notice, on a worldwide battlefield." According to human rights group Reprieve, well over a thousand people, many of them children, have been killed in Pakistan and Yemen during attempts to kill just 41 men.[10]

Said Lt. Gen. Michael Flynn, former head of the Defense Intelligence Agency: "Our entire Middle East policy seems to be based on firing drones...They're enamored by the ability of special operations and the CIA to find a guy in the middle of the desert in some shitty little village and drop a bomb on his head and kill him."[11]

Josh Earnest, the White House spokesman, assured us that "If necessary, the President would implement changes that would make tragedies like this one less likely to occur in the future."[12] But these are empty words. Professor Marc Herold's research has shown that "as the U.S. bombs get smarter, civilian casualties increase." The military is encouraged to "drop bombs on sites which previously might not have been hit for fear of causing widespread civilian deaths."[13]

## Terrorism[14]

Polls[15] show that Americans are more afraid of a terrorist attack than at any other time since 9/11, even though the *rate of violent crime has been consistently dropping* since 1993,[16] and even though the annual number of violent jihadist attacks in the U.S. since 9/11 is about the same as the number of Americans killed by toddlers.[17]

Yet a Fox News analyst called ISIS "the single biggest threat in [America's] 200-year history."[18] The national news media has driven Americans to a frenzy of fear, leaving more and more of them to express their concerns, even though the threat of attack *IN* the U.S. is less than the threat of attack *BY* the U.S.

The Air Force is dropping so many bombs on Muslim countries that companies like Boeing are gearing up for increased weaponry sales, as stock prices for weapons manufacturers keep surging.[19]

And our nation keeps building up the stock of arms around the world. In 2014 alone, arms sales increased 35 percent, to $36.2 billion.[20]

## Weapons for ISIS—from US!

According to the Stockholm International Peace Research Institute (SIPRI), the USA has sold or donated major arms to at least 96 nations in the past five years.[21] Here again, our political leaders ignore us. Most voters favor defense cuts, but most politicians don't.[22]

The weapons we sell to Saudi Arabia are destroying the villages of Yemen, killing entire families and leveling their homes.[23] As Glenn Greenwald notes, "You'll almost never hear any of those victims' names on CNN, NPR, or most other large U.S. media outlets…You'll never know anything about them—not even their names, let alone hear about their extinguished life aspirations or hear from their grieving survivors."[24]

It has been reported that ISIS has confiscated large numbers of weapons from Saudi Arabia, which has become the **Number 1 U.S. customer for arms sales**, as well as the world's Number 1 importer of weapons.[25]

We could ultimately be victims of our own aggression. The *World Protests* report concluded that the most recent decade represents one of the most agitated periods in modern history—comparable to pre-Civil War days, World War I, and the Civil Rights era.[26] According to expert Scott Atran, terrorism primarily appeals to young men who are bored and underemployed; for them, "jihad is an egalitarian, equal-opportunity employer."[27] Mercy Corps added, "Young people take up the gun not because they are poor, but because they are angry."[28] Their terrorist acts may not take a conventional form. Public health expert Dr. Ali Khan notes, "A deadly microbe like smallpox—to which we no longer have immunity—can be easily recreated in a rogue laboratory."[29]

## Disposable Soldiers

With more drone warfare and fewer "boots on the ground," fewer young Americans are being killed. But disposability takes other forms. Rather than heaping faint praise on our young soldiers as they go off to fight for our "freedom," we should be teaching them about their likely roles in the killing machine.

In her book, *They Were Soldiers: How the Wounded Return from America's Wars—The Untold Story*, Ann Jones recounted the experience of a doctor in Afghanistan: "His first surgical patient…was a young soldier who had stepped on an IED, triggering an upward blast that destroyed his legs and left his pelvic cavity 'hollowed out.' His urinary system was in shreds. His testicles were destroyed. His penis was attached to his body by only 'a little thread of skin.' That first surgery, the doctor said, was 'emotional' for everyone on the surgical team. 'The others hadn't seen anything like these injuries for a while, and I had never seen anything like it.'"[30]

The aftereffects of war can be equally devastating. Over a third of American troops returning from Iraq and Afghanistan have been diagnosed with PTSD and other mental disorders, more often than not the youngest soldiers, little more than children.[31] Thousands come home with cancers and respiratory diseases from the use or disposal of toxic chemicals and medical waste.[32] Veterans are much more likely than other citizens to be unemployed, or, much worse, to commit suicide. And tens of thousands of homeless veterans are walking the streets (although Connecticut, Virginia, Philadelphia, San Diego, New Orleans and other locations have made progress in housing them).[33]

## The "Freedom" Illusion

War and "freedom" have always been interconnected in American history. Abraham Lincoln spoke of the Civil War as "a new birth of freedom," World War II had FDR's "Four Freedoms" and the pro-war "Fight for Freedom Committee." The Cold War was waged to defend the "Free World." The Iraq War was labeled "Operation Iraqi Freedom." After 9/11, President George W. Bush told America: "Freedom itself is under attack...They hate our freedoms."

But the U.S. military, says a special report from the *LA Times*, "is gradually becoming a separate warrior class...that is becoming increasingly distinct from the public it is charged with protecting."[34] Almost half of our 1.3 million active-duty troops come from just five states (California, Virginia, Texas, North Carolina and Georgia), and only a quarter of Americans admit to closely following news of war.[35]

War does not bring freedom. In some ways, it defies freedom. In 1778, the Continental Congress created a whistleblower protection law[36] that affirmed "the duty of all persons in the service of the United States to give the earliest information to Congress or other proper authority of any misconduct, frauds, or misdemeanors committed by any officers or persons in the service of these states." But whistleblowers Edward Snowden (spying), Chelsea Manning (war crimes), John Kiriakou (torture), and the *Drone Papers* author have never been afforded the freedom to educate the American public about military abuses.

## Personal: Soldiers[37]

Drone operator Brandon Bryant's first strike was in Afghanistan, where three alleged Taliban members were walking along the road, starting and stopping, constantly looking around, perhaps nervous about being out in the open in a frequently targeted area. Thousands of miles away, a button was pushed, and the screen in front of Bryant turned suddenly white, as from a camera flash. Then stillness. He says he'll never forget the moment: "The smoke clears, and there's pieces of the two guys around the crater. And there's this guy over here, and he's missing his right leg above his knee. He's holding it, and he's rolling around, and the blood is squirting out of his leg, and it's hitting the ground, and it's hot. His blood is hot. But when it hits the ground, it starts to cool off; the pool cools fast. It took him a long time to die. I just watched him. I watched him become the same color as the ground he was lying on."

The other drone operators celebrated their colleague's first kill.

Bryant's second strike came after he and another operator had been monitoring the compound of a high-level Taliban or al Qaeda official. They watched for hours, observing nothing but goats and cows grazing near the mud-brick structure. Finally, they were ordered to level the building. Just before impact, Bryant detected a movement at the side of the compound. "This figure runs around the corner, the outside, toward the front of the building. And it looked like a little kid to me. Like a little human person." Once again, a silent white flash filled the computer screen. Bryant paused, then turned to his partner: "Did that look like a child to you?"

Bryant's next strike targeted five individuals traveling with a camel through a mountain pass between Pakistan and Afghanistan. They were suspected of transporting explosives. But Bryant was uneasy; the men didn't appear to be carrying weapons, and the bags on the camel did not betray the bulk of smuggled arms. At dusk, the men made their beds for the night, and soon after, with a command from the drone operator's screen, a Hellfire missile was released, and the resting men were obliterated. There was no chain reaction, as might have been expected from concealed explosives on the ground. Said Bryant, "We waited for those men to settle down in their beds and then we killed them in their sleep."

The turnover rate for Air Force drone operators is unmanageably high, for at least three reasons. First, the operators are overworked, putting in 12-hour days, with few days off. Second, they are dismissed as second-class airmen by the real pilots. "We were looked down upon, because we were wearing flight suits but not sitting in the cockpit of an actual aircraft. Drones were like a joke in the military." Third, and likely most significantly, many drone operators were devastated by the horror of it all, by the bloody destruction they triggered at their keyboards. A drone analyst asked, "How many women and children have you seen incinerated by a Hellfire missile? How many men have you seen crawl across a field, trying to make it to the nearest compound for help while bleeding out from severed legs?"

The military takes its drone business seriously. In early 2016, 59-year-old activist Grady Flores began a six-month sentence for taking photographs of a peaceful protest outside a drone training center near Syracuse, New York. Flores was influenced by the 2013 testimony of a Pakistani man whose mother was killed by a drone while she was outside picking vegetables with her grandchildren. "Now," says Flores, "the kids live in terror."

## Notes

1  Burns, Ken, *The Civil War*. Public Broadcasting System.
2  McElroy, John, *Andersonville: A Story of Rebel Military Prisons*. Washington, *The National Tribune*, 1899 [c1879].
3  Civil War Transcript, Library of Congress (www.loc.gov/today/cyberlc/transcripts/2013/130227mus1200.txt), accessed February 20, 2016; "War Letters." *American Experience*, Public Broadcasting System; "Death and the Civil War." *American Experience*, Public Broadcasting System.

4 "My Lai." *American Experience*, Public Broadcasting System.

5 Buchheit, Paul, "How America Invites Terrorism." NationOfChange.org, June 8, 2015; Buchheit, Paul, "Nine Numbers That Cry Out: 'Bring on Bernie!'" CommonDreams.org, December 21, 2015; Buchheit, Paul, "Five New Year's Resolutions for Cognitively-Deprived Conservatives." CommonDreams.org, December 28, 2015.

6 "The President's 2017 Budget Proposal in Pictures." National Priorities Project, February 17, 2016; "The State of America's Children." Children's Defense Fund, 2014.

7 Turse, Nick, "Iraq, Afghanistan, and Other Special Ops 'Successes': America's Elite Forces Deploy to a Record-Shattering 147 Countries in 2015." TomDispatch.com, October 26, 2015.

8 Coll, Steve, "The Unblinking Stare." *The New Yorker*, November 24, 2014.

9 "The Drone Papers." *The Intercept*.

10 "You Never Die Twice." Reprieve.org, 2014.

11 "The Drone Papers: Find, Fix, Finish." *The Intercept*.

12 Shear, Michael D. and Senguptaoct, Somini, "Obama Issues Rare Apology Over Bombing of Doctors Without Borders Hospital in Afghanistan." *New York Times*, October 7, 2015.

13 Herold, Marc, "Our Modern Military Warfare Only Kills the 'Bad Guys.'" In Buchheit, Paul, *American Wars, Illusions & Realities,* Clarity Press, 2008.

14 "Freedom in the World." Freedom House, 2015; "Democracy Index 2012." *The Economist* Intelligence Unit, 2012; "Global Militarization Index." Bonn International Center for Conversion, 2014; "SIPRI Arms Transfers Database." Stockholm International Peace Research Institute, 2015; "Global Wealth Databook." Credit Suisse Research Institute Publications, 2015.

15 Chan, Melissa, "Americans Are More Fearful of Terrorism Than Any Other Time Since Sept. 11." *Time*, December 10, 2015; Murray, Mark, "ISIS Threat: Fear of Terror Attack Soars to 9/11 High, NBC News/WSJ Poll Finds." NBC News, September 9, 2014.

16 "Criminal Victimization, 2013." U.S. Department of Justice, September 19, 2014.

17 Sanburn, Josh, "This Is How Often Toddlers Shoot People By Mistake." *Time*, April 28, 2016; Ingraham, Christopher, "People are Getting Shot By Toddlers on a Weekly Basis This Year." *Washington Post*, October 14, 2015; "Deadly Attacks Since 9/11." *International Security*.

18 "Judge Jeanine: ISIS Is Coming to Our Soil and We Are Not Ready." Fox News, September 21, 2014.

19 Vanden Brook, Tom, "Air Force Burning through Bomb Stockpiles Striking ISIL." *USA Today*, December 3, 2015.

20 Nicks, Denver, "The U.S. Is Still No.1 at Selling Arms to the World." *Time*, December 26, 2015.

21 "Asia and the Middle East Lead Rise in Arms Imports; the United States and Russia Remain Largest Arms Exporters, Says SIPRI." Stockholm International Peace Research Institute, February 2016.

22 Chadwick, Lauren, "Most Voters Favor Defense Cuts. Most Politicians Don't." *Time*, March 10, 2016.

23 Craig, Iona, "The Agony of Saada." *The Intercept*, November 16, 2015.

24 Greenwald, Glenn, "Highlighting Western Victims While Ignoring Victims of Western Violence." *The Intercept*, March 25, 2016.

25 "Saudi Arabia Becomes World's Top Arms Importer." RT.com, March 9, 2015.

26 "World Protests Report." Initiative for Policy Dialogue, 2013.

27 Hasan, Mehdi, "What the Jihadists Who Bought 'Islam for Dummies' on Amazon Tell Us about Radicalisation." *New Statesman*, August 21, 2014.

28 "Injustice, Not Unemployment, a Key Driver of Youth Participation in Violence." Mercy Corps, February 17, 2015.

29 Khan, Ali and Patrick, William, "Forget Zika—the Flu is the Greatest Threat of All." *New York Post*, June 11, 2016.

30 Jones, Ann, *They Were Soldiers: How the Wounded Return from America's Wars—The Untold Story*. Haymarket Books/Dispatch Books, 2013.

31 Lowe, Christian, "Mental Illness Plagues Current Vets." Military.com, March 14, 2007.

32 Hickman, Joseph, *The Burn Pits: The Poisoning of America's Soldiers*. Little City Books, 2016.

33 Fifield, Jen, "Cities, States Fight Veteran Homelessness." Pew Charitable Trusts, December 21, 2015.

34 Zucchino, David and Cloud, David S., "US Military and Civilians Are Increasingly Divided." *LA Times*, May 24, 2015.

35 "War and Sacrifice in the Post-9/11 Era: The Military-Civilian Gap." Pew Research Center, October 5, 2011.

36 Van Buren, Peter, "Welcome to Post-Constitution America." *The Nation*, August 5, 2013.

37 Pilkington, Ed, "Life as a Drone Operator." *The Guardian*, November 19, 2015; Power, Matthew, "Confessions of a Drone Warrior." GQ, October 22, 2013; Chatterjee, Pratap, "American Drone Operators Are Quitting in Record Numbers." *The Nation*, March 5, 2015; Moyers, Bill, "A Drone Protestor Heads to Jail." CommonDreams.org, January 21, 2016.

## Bibliography

Buchheit, Paul (Ed.), *American Wars, Illusions & Realities*. Clarity Press, 2008.

Burrowes, Robert J., *The Rule of Law: Unjust and Violent*. Information Clearing House, August 15, 2013.

Chomsky, Noam, *Because We Say So*. City Lights Open Media, 2015.

Giroux, Henry A., *America's Addiction to Terrorism*. Monthly Review Press, 2016.

Hartmann, Thom, *What Would Jefferson Do?* Broadway Books, 2005.

Hedges, Chris, *War Is a Force that Gives Us Meaning*. Anchor, 2003.

Hickman, Joseph, *The Burn Pits: The Poisoning of America's Soldiers*. Little City Books, 2016.

Jones, Ann, *They Were Soldiers: How the Wounded Return from America's Wars—The Untold Story*. Haymarket Books/Dispatch Books, 2013.

McElroy, John, *Andersonville: A Story of Rebel Military Prisons*. Washington, *The National Tribune*, 1899 [c1879].

McHenry, Keith, *Hungry for Peace: How You Can Help End Poverty and War with Food Not Bombs*. Sharp Press, 2011.

Mehta, Vijay, *The Economics of Killing*. Pluto Press, 2012.

Roach, Mary, *Grunt: The Curious Science of Humans at War*. W.W. Norton, 2016.

Scahill, Jeremy, *The Assassination Complex: Inside the Government's Secret Drone Warfare Program*. Simon & Schuster, 2016.

Williams, David, *A People's History of the Civil War*. The New Press, 2006.

# 15

# AMERICIDE[1]

Based on a study of 1,779 policy issues, Princeton researchers Martin Gilens and Benjamin I. Page concluded that "the preferences of the average American appear to have only a minuscule, near-zero, statistically non-significant impact upon public policy."[2]

Americans in the middle and lower classes, the vulnerable women, children, elderly and people of color, are generally ignored by politicians, business leaders, and the mainstream media. But these are the people who need to be heard. These are the beaten-down Americans who deserve the right to dignified lives in the richest country in the history of the world.

A summary of *Americide*, the economic, physical, mental, and emotional disposing of Americans:

## The Black American

> I cringed when people would ask me where I lived…Just to say 'public housing' was basically saying that you're dirty, you're bad, you're dumb, you're lazy, you're a problem.
>
> Shana griffin, New Orleans activist[3]

Emergency home repairs? Not for black families. The average African-American family had readily available liquid wealth of only $200 in 2011, less than $1 for every $100 owned by whites.[4]

We tend to believe that education is the great equalizer. But a middle-aged black person with a *graduate degree* has about the same odds of being a millionaire as a white person with only a high school diploma.[5]

## The Child

My little sister. She's hungry.

An Ohio boy, sifting through his school's garbage bin[6]

For every THREE homeless children in 2006, there are now FIVE.[7] For every THREE children on food stamps in 2007, there are now FIVE.[8]

And yet spending on children's programs recently declined for the first time in nearly 20 years.[9]

## The Senior Citizen

I am over 60, and I was pushed out of my job because of my age. My rent, car note, and electricity are all two months behind. I can barely get food. Utilities will be cut off soon.

A Laurel, Maryland senior citizen[10]

With the average cost of a year's worth of life-preserving drugs over $50,000, 43 percent of sick Americans skipped doctor's visits and/or medication purchases in 2011–12 because of excessive costs.[11] It keeps getting worse. About half of households age 55 and older have no 401(k) or IRA or other retirement savings.[12]

## The Young Adult

I was denied the license to practice in my profession because of my student loans…I make $8.50 an hour as a cashier at ACE Hardware.

Hilary, a student[13]

Over one generation, from 1984 to 2009, the net worth of an American under 35 dropped from $11,521 to $3,662, a **68 percent decline**, in good part because of debt. In approximately the same time, the percentage of stay-at-home young adults rose from 11 percent to almost 24 percent.[14]

Just get a job at Apple? The company makes a $400,000 profit per employee[15] while paying its retail specialists less than $30,000 per year.[16]

## The Veteran

*This figure runs around the corner…it looked like a little kid to me. A silent white flash filled the computer screen.* Bryant paused, then turned to his partner. *Did that look like a child to you?*

Brandon Bryant, former drone operator[17]

Over a third of American troops returning from Iraq and Afghanistan have been diagnosed with some sort of mental disorder.[18] Yet, from 1970 to 2002, the per capita number of public mental health hospital beds plummeted from 207 per 100,000 to 21 per 100,000[19]—nearly a *90 percent cut!* After the recession, state funding was cut some more.[20]

## The American Woman

> My husband lost his job...I graduated from a four-year nursing school... but I have been unable to find a nursing job and was working part time... my student loans are all in deferral...I am expecting to give birth in one month, so I can't get a second job.
>
> Woman in Bergenfield, NJ[21]

Women earn just 80 percent of men's pay,[22] and they have barely half the retirement assets of men.[23]

But women are earning more undergraduate degrees than men, more master's degrees than men, and more PhDs than men.[24]

## The Renter

> I have enough money to last about a month before I go homeless...a year-long waiting list for any housing assistance. I have nowhere to turn.
>
> Renter in Missoula, Montana[25]

According to the Census Bureau, median income has dropped by 6.5 percent since 2007.[26] But rents keep going up. As a result, the number of families spending more than half their incomes on rent—the "severely" cost-burdened renters—has surged from 7.5 million to 11.4 million in the last decade, a stunning 50 percent increase.[27]

Billionaire Steve Schwarzman[28] finds the growing anger among voters "astonishing." But his company, Blackstone, is a corporate model for making money at the expense of desperate former homeowners. Since the recession, it has become the nation's leading landlord,[29] buying up tens of thousands of homes at rock-bottom prices, and then renting them back, often to the very people who lost them.[30]

What is truly "astonishing" is that people like Schwarzman fail to see—or refuse to see—what their lust for money is doing to beaten-down Americans.

## Notes

1   Buchheit, Paul, "Americide." Commondreams.org, January 19, 2015.

2 Gilens, Martin and Page, Benjamin I., "Testing Theories of American Politics: Elites, Interest Groups, and Average Citizens." *Perspectives on Politics*, September 2014.

3 McClain, Dani, "How New Orleans Has Lost 1/3 of its Black Population: Policies to Make People Disappear." Alternet.org, November 3, 2015.

4 "Beyond Broke," *Duke Center for Global Policy Solutions*, April, 2014.

5 Stilwell, Victoria, "What Are Your Odds of Becoming a Millionaire?" Bloomberg Business, January 21, 2016.

6 "The Early Childhood Hunger ImperaTive." Children's Defense Fund, January 2016.

7 "America's Youngest Outcasts: A Report Card on Child Homelessness." Homelesschildrenamerica.org, November 2014.

8 "One in Five Children Receive Food Stamps." U.S. Census Bureau, February 20, 2015.

9 "Survey Finds Decline in Child Welfare Spending." Child Trends, September 26, 2014.

10 Center for Effective Government (www.foreffectivegov.org/reports/), accessed November 14, 2016.

11 "43 Percent of U.S. Working-Age Adults Can't Afford Doctor." UPI, April 26, 2013.

12 "Most Households Approaching Retirement Have Low Savings." Government Accountability Office, May 12, 2015.

13 "The Most Depressing Student Loan Stories." *Daily Finance*, September 20, 2012.

14 Frey, Richard and Passel, Jeffrey S., "In Post-Recession Era, Young Adults Drive Continuing Rise in Multi-Generational Living." Pew Research Center, July 17, 2014.

15 Worstall, Tim, "More Than 90% Of US Businesses Don't Pay the Corporate Income Tax." Forbes, December 23, 2014.

16 "Apple Salaries." Glassdoor.com, Updated in March 2016.

17 Power, Matthew, "Confessions of a Drone Warrior." GQ, October 22, 2013.

18 Lowe, Christian, "Mental Illness Plagues Current Vets." Military.com, March 14, 2007.

19 Yoon, Jangho and Bruckner, Tim A., "Does Deinstitutionalization Increase Suicide?" Health Services Research, August 2009.

20 "State Mental Health Cuts: The Continuing Crisis." National Alliance on Mental Illness, November 2011.

21 Center for Effective Government (www.foreffectivegov.org/reports/), accessed November 14, 2016.

22 "20 Facts about U.S. Inequality that Everyone Should Know." The Stanford Center on Poverty and Inequality.

23 Sweetland Edwards, Haley, "Why Can't Drug Costs Be Reined In?" *Time*, May 19, 2016.

24 "The Rise of Women: Seven Charts Showing Women's Rapid Gains in Educational Achievement." Russell Sage Foundation, February 21, 2013.

25 Center for Effective Government (www.foreffectivegov.org/reports/), accessed November 14, 2016.

26 "Income, Poverty and Health Insurance Coverage in the United States: 2014." U.S. Census Bureau, September 16, 2015.

27 Olick, Diana, "Housing's New Crisis: Half Your Income for Rent." CNBC, December 9, 2015.

28 Sherman, Erik, "Blackstone CEO Surprised American Voters Are Unhappy with Economy, Politics, Life." Forbes, January 21, 2016.

29 Perlberg, Heather and Gittelsohn, John, "Wall Street Unlocks Profits from Distress with Rental Revolution." Bloomberg Business, December 19, 2013.

30 Edelman, Sarah, "When Wall Street Buys Main Street." Center for American Progress, February 27, 2014.

# 16

# THE CASE FOR A GUARANTEED INCOME

The concept of a Basic Income in the U.S. goes back to Thomas Paine, one of the driving forces for independence and equality during the American Revolution. Support over the years has come from sources as diverse as Martin Luther King, who led an all-out attack on poverty, and Milton Friedman, who advocated a negative income tax that would subsidize low-earning taxpayers.[1] Richard Nixon backed Friedman's ideas. Staunch conservative Charles Murray proposed eliminating Social Security and Medicare in favor of a cash grant to every adult.[2]

A World Bank analysis of 19 studies found that *Cash transfers have been demonstrated to improve education and health outcomes and alleviate poverty... concerns about the use of cash transfers for alcohol and tobacco consumption are unfounded.*[3] An MIT/Harvard analysis of seven cash transfer trials found "no systematic evidence that cash transfer programs discourage work."[4] The Brooks World Poverty Institute found that money transfers to the poor are used primarily for basic needs.[5] Basic Incomes have been shown to lead to reductions in crime, inequality, malnutrition and infant mortality.[6] The uncertainty of irregular incomes, on the other hand, is associated with a significant decline in cognitive ability,[7] and, as discussed earlier, with an increase in stress and anxiety.

One of the earliest experiments with guaranteed incomes was the Mincome (minimum income) program conducted in the town of Dauphin, Manitoba during the 1970s.[8] The results were never made clear, partly because of a change to a more conservative government, which put the program's records in storage, unevaluated. One study, however, found improved health outcomes for the recipients of the basic income payments.[9] Today in Canada, the mayors of two cities in right-leaning Alberta are considering a renewal of the guaranteed income concept.

Back in the U.S., the Alaska Permanent Fund[10] has thrived for 35 years, even with anti-socialist conservatives in power. Texas has long employed a Permanent School Fund to distribute funds from mineral rights to the public education system. Wyoming has used a similar Mineral Trust Fund to help eliminate state income taxes. Nebraska distributes low-cost electricity from a publicly owned utility. Oregon has used the proceeds from wind energy to return hundreds of dollars to households. Vermont has proposed a Common Assets Trust to raise money from taxes on pollution and pay dividends to residents. A pilot basic income experiment is set to begin in Oakland.[11]

Numerous Native American communities have instituted guaranteed income programs, both in the form of shared benefits from casinos and as "land trusts," which recognize the common ownership of natural resources.[12] Notably, according to a Duke University analysis, the establishment of the Eastern Cherokee Indian Land Trust[13] has resulted in fewer behavioral and emotional problems among the community's children, relative to neighboring communities. In adulthood, recipients had less depression, anxiety, and alcohol dependence.[14]

As noted earlier, a 2005 program in Britain[15] demonstrated that the increase of family income, especially through work opportunities, resulted in "more spending on family needs and less on alcohol and tobacco." A broader study of 18 European countries[16] showed that dividend payments encourage people to work harder, rather than to waste their time and money. Now Finland is readying a wide-scale guaranteed income program, and cities in the Netherlands are preparing similar experiments with such "basic income" payments.[17] Despite an initial rejection of a basic income proposal, citizens of Switzerland continue to advocate for a Guaranteed Income plan that would provide $2,600 a month tax-free to every adult, and $650 to each child.[18]

In Brazil, Bolsa Família, the largest cash transfer program in the world, has dramatically reduced poverty, although corrupt national leadership may be reversing the trend.[19]

A program in Uganda followed young people who were given cash grants with twice the typical annual income. After four years, most had invested their earnings in vocations, causing their earnings to rise by 40 percent or more, an outcome that generally lasted well beyond the four-year study period. Women overall earned more than men. As summarized by the authors of the study, "The grants are typically invested and yield high returns…even among poor, unemployed and relatively uneducated women."[20]

In Namibia, a two-year program yielded remarkable results, reducing poverty from 76 percent to 16 percent, child malnutrition from 42 percent to 10 percent, and school dropout rates from 40 percent to almost zero. A Unicef-funded study in India recorded the same positive health effects, with particularly noticeable improvements among the disabled population.

The charity Give Directly, which has been highly rated by the charity research organization GiveWell, provided cash transfers to poor rural households in

Kenya. Results showed increased spending on food, medical needs, and education, with very little used for alcohol and tobacco, and with similar outcomes for both males and females. According to the authors of the study, "Transfer recipients experience large increases in psychological well-being."[21]

Even the concept of providing grants to homeless people seems to work.[22] In both Utah and California, trial programs have led to stable living conditions for dozens of formerly homeless people, with few conflicts or behavioral issues within the communities, and at a significantly lower cost than the alternative of temporary shelters—especially if people without homes are given jobs, as in a new program in Albuquerque.[23]

Beyond the practical benefits are other factors that urge longer-term acceptance of the Guaranteed Income. People thrive on equality and stability in their daily lives. And on sharing with others. As stated by author Peter Linebaugh, "Scarcely a society has existed on the face of the earth which has not had at its heart the commons."[24]

The Universal Declaration of Emergent Human Rights[25] confirms the right to a basic income, the "aim of which is to put an end to poverty and social exclusion." People need a minimum income to ensure security and contentment in their lives. The controversial "Easterlin Paradox,"[26] which suggests that happiness is not correlated with income increases beyond approximately $75,000, was clarified by an NIH study that found no heightening of "emotional well-being" (related to life experiences) after that income plateau had been reached.[27]

The Guaranteed Income concept is not a left–right issue, it is not welfare for the poor or the rich, it is not blessing or bane to any exclusive segment of America. Whereas liberals see it as a means of lifting millions of Americans out of poverty, conservatives and libertarians endorse it as a means of decreasing government intervention and promoting individual choice in spending decisions.

## It Can Be Funded

Admittedly, funding may not be sufficient at first to provide a living income for every American family. Yet even implemented incrementally, the stimulus resulting from the initiative and entrepreneurship of middle- to lower-income recipients will advance the process. Various means of funding stand out:

- **Collecting from Corporate Tax Avoiders**. Citizens for Tax Justice recently reported that Fortune 500 companies are holding $2.4 trillion in accumulated profits offshore for tax purposes, with estimated taxes due of nearly $700 billion.[28] That's about $5,000 per household. Oxfam says tax dodging by multinational corporations costs the U.S. approximately $111 billion each year.[29] Yet, even though every hour worked by an IRS auditor uncovers over $9,000 in misreported tax dollars among large corporations,[30] IRS staff have been steadily cut back as the wealthiest Americans build up their fortunes, forcing communities around the nation to rely on regressive property and sales taxes to make up the difference.

- **Collecting from Individual Tax Avoiders**. According to a recent IRS report,[31] an incredible $406 billion annual gap exists between owed and paid taxes, with individuals accounting for over three-quarters of the total, and with the most egregious misreporting coming from the highest income-takers.[32] That's about $3,000 per U.S. household in annual lost revenue. In another analysis, the Tax Justice Network estimates that from $21 trillion to $32 trillion is being hoarded untaxed by the global elite.[33] The recently published *Panama Papers* are beginning to show the details.[34] Considering that over a third of global wealth is owned by Americans, it can be estimated that up to $10 trillion of U.S. wealth is untaxed, and that a one-time 35 percent tax on these funds would generate $3.5 trillion, or $10,000 for every man, woman, and child in the United States.[35]

- **A Financial Speculation Tax**. Also called a Financial Transaction Tax[36] and a Robin Hood Tax,[37] it is a very small sales charge on Wall Street transactions, perhaps half of one percent on stock trades, with the potential to return up to $300–400 billion in revenue every year.[38] The logic for the tax is indisputable: (1) The financial industry, which was responsible for the speculation and fraud that devastated middle-class homeowner wealth, generates 30 percent of U.S. corporate profits, but only pays 18 percent of the corporate federal taxes;[39] (2) U.S. investors pay zero sales tax on their speculative transactions; and (3) The tax is easy to implement, and has been successful in other countries. In late 2015, ten European countries (Germany, France, Italy, Austria, Belgium, Greece, Portugal, Slovakia, Slovenia and Spain) agreed on aspects of a tax that could make it a reality within a year.[40]

- **Military Cuts**. Nationally, we spend over $1 trillion per year on defense.[41] Not just the half-trillion Pentagon budget, but another half-trillion for veterans' affairs, homeland security, "contingency operations," and a variety of other miscellaneous military "necessities," with hundreds of billions of dollars in wasteful, unaccountable spending.[42] Most Americans favor cuts to nuclear weapons, ground forces, and questionable air power projects like the F-35.[43]

- **A Progressive Income Tax**. Just 12 to 20 percent in taxes for all the privileges America heaps upon wealthy individuals and corporations?[44] The prominent economic team of Piketty and Saez and Stantcheva determined that "the top tax rate could potentially be set as high as 83%" before the highest earners are discouraged from attempting to earn more.[45] Other economists go further,[46] up to 90 percent, and even some conservative analysts[47] concede that the optimal maximum may be at least 50 percent. Importantly, higher taxes won't make rich people leave. A Stanford study concluded that "higher income earners show greater residential stability and geographic embeddedness than do low income earners."[48]

- **Revising Regressive and Other Unfair Tax Structures**. A payroll tax that primarily impacts low earners, an almost nonexistent *estate tax*, and a lower *capital gains* rate on carried interest for investment managers are all indirect forms of tax avoidance by wealthy Americans. It is estimated that $300 billion in annual revenue would be realized just by eliminating the ceiling on the *payroll tax*, for which a $35,000 secretary pays 6.2 percent and a $500,000 lawyer just 1.5 percent.[49]

- **A Wealth Tax**, as recommended by Thomas Piketty,[50] based on the belief, as outlined earlier, that wealth is created by a cooperating society of people, rather than by a single individual or corporation. According to an Institute for Policy Studies report, a one percent wealth tax on the richest one percent of Americans would generate $260 billion annually, over $2,000 per U.S. household.[51]

- **A Carbon Tax**.[52] Every year, human activity dumps over 30 billion tons of $CO_2$ into the air, most certainly contributing to the dramatic rise in global warming. Yet, instead of demanding payment from the biggest polluters, we give them subsidies of over $5 trillion per year, more than the combined health care budget of all the nations in the world. The U.S. is also ranked near the bottom of the world in compensation from corporations for their oil and gas extraction.

- **A Land Tax**. This goes back to Thomas Paine, who said "Every proprietor… of cultivated lands, owes to the community ground-rent." The greatest proponent was Henry George,[53] who was supported by such varied notables as Adam Smith, Milton Friedman, Winston Churchill, the Organisation for Economic Co-operation and Development, the International Monetary Fund, and the Institute of Fiscal Studies.

- **Patent Reform**. As noted earlier, corporations take out government-protected patents—for 20 years—on products developed with U.S. taxpayer dollars. Robert Reich sensibly calls for a shortening of the patent duration, or, instead, a fair return to U.S. citizens for the decades of research that have led to billions in profits.[54]

- **A Share of the Research Benefits**. Mariana Mazzucato reminds us that the U.S. used to retain interest in government-funded companies such as Bell Labs.[55] As discussed earlier, the majority of basic research is still coming from the U.S. taxpayers.

- **Safety Net Savings**. Programs for the poor cost our nation anywhere from $606 billion to $742 billion per year.[56] That's up to $6,000 per household. A Demos study calculated that a national dividend of $3,000 a year ($9,000 for a typical family) could potentially cut poverty in half.[57]

Many of these ideas are similar to those of the "Just Third Way" movement[58] of the Center for Economic and Social Justice, which would provide a guaranteed income through a "Capital Homestead Account."[59]

The main argument for a Guaranteed Income is that we've all contributed to American prosperity, through our own labors or that of our parents and grandparents. The combination of modern technology, financial deregulation and wealth-favoring tax law has allowed a relatively few savvy professionals to redirect our national wealth with an alacrity and dexterity that easily outpaces our slowly evolving society. A Guaranteed Income would address this in a manner unobjectionable to almost everyone. Ultimately, it will demonstrate the value of people too long considered disposable.

## Notes

1 Gordon, Noah, "The Conservative Case for a Guaranteed Basic Income." *The Atlantic*, August 6, 2014; de Rugy, Veronica, "Time for a Guaranteed Income?" Reason.com, February 19, 2014.

2 Murray, Charles, "A Guaranteed Income for Every American." *Wall Street Journal*, June 3, 2016.

3 Evans, David K. and Popova, Anna, "Cash Transfers and Temptation Goods: A Review of Global Evidence." The World Bank, May 1, 2014.

4 Banerjee, Abhijit; Hanna, Rema; Kreindler, Gabriel; and Olken, Benjamin, "Debunking the Stereotype of the Lazy Welfare Recipient." HKS Working Paper No. 076, December 14, 2015.

5 Hanlon, Joseph; Barrientos, Armando; and Hulme, David, *Just Give Money to the Poor: The Development Revolution from the Global South*. Kumarian Press, 2010.

6 "About Basic Income." *Basic Income* (BasicIncome.org).

7 Marquiél, Jean-Claude; Tucker, Philip; Folkard, Simon; Gentil, Catherine; Ansiau, David: "Chronic Effects of Shift Work on Cognition: Findings from the VISAT Longitudinal Study Press Release." *Occupational and Environmental Medicine*, November 3, 2014.

8 Lum, Zi-Ann, "A Canadian City Once Eliminated Poverty and Nearly Everyone Forgot About It." *Huffington Post*, December 23, 2014.

9 Forget, Evelyn L., "The Town with No Poverty." University of Manitoba, February 2011; Surowiecki, James, "The Case for Free Money: Why Don't We Have Universal Basic Income?" *The New Yorker*, June 20, 2016.

10 The Alaska Permanent Fund Corporation, apfc.org.

11 Conger, Kate, "Y Combinator Announces Basic Income Pilot Experiment in Oakland." *TechCrunch*, May 31, 2016.

12 "Native American Trust Lands Explained." *1st Tribal Lending*, accessed 2016.

13 Eastern Cherokee Indian Land Trust (Qualla Boundary). *Wikipedia*, accessed 2016.

14 Costello, Jane, "Many Countries are Weighing Cash Payments to Citizens. Could it work in the U.S.?" *Salon*, June 21, 2016.

15 Waldfogel, Jane, "Tackling Child Poverty & Improving Child Well-Being: Lessons from Britain." Columbia University & London School of Economics, December 2010.

16  van der Wel, Kjetil A. and Halvorsen, Knut, "The Bigger the Worse? A Comparative Study of the Welfare State and Employment Commitment." Oslo and Akershus University College of Applied Sciences, Norway, November 25, 2014.

17  Oltermann, Philip, "State Handouts for All? Europe Set to Pilot Universal Basic Incomes." *The Guardian*, June 2, 2016; Diez, Maria Sanchez, "A Dutch city is Giving Money away to Test the 'Basic Income' Theory." *Quartz*, June 30, 2015.

18  Bachmann, Helena, "Global first? Every Swiss Could be Guaranteed $2,600 a Month Tax-Free." *USA Today*, May 5, 2016; "Switzerland's Voters Reject Basic Income Plan." BBC News, June 5, 2016; Jourdan, Stanislas, "Europe: 64% of People in Favour of Basic Income, Poll Finds." Basic Income Earth Network, May 22, 2016; Santens, Scott, "The Results of the Basic Income Referendum in Switzerland." medium.com, June 6, 2016.

19  Pizzigati, Sam, "In Brazil, a Pre-Olympics Folly." Inequality.org, July 21, 2016; Ortiz, Fabiola, "Fiscal Austerity May Jeopardize Brazil's Poverty Alleviation Program." Truthout.org, September 27, 2015.

20  Blattman, Christopher; Fiala, Nathan; Martinez, Sebastian: "Generating Skilled Self-Employment in Developing Countries: Experimental Evidence from Uganda." *Quarterly Journal of Economics*, November 14, 2013.

21  GiveDirectly.org; GiveWell.org.

22  Carrier, Scott, "Room for Improvement." *Mother Jones*, March/April 2015; Sanburn, Josh, "The Radically Simple Solution to Homelessness." *Time*, March 3, 2016.

23  "Albuquerque Mayor: Here's a Crazy Idea, Let's Give Homeless People Jobs." PBS *News Hour*, November 26, 2015.

24  Linebaugh, Peter, *Stop, Thief!: The Commons, Enclosures, and Resistance.* PM Press, 2014.

25  *Universal Declaration of Emergent Human Rights.* Barcelona2004.org.

26  Easterlin, Richard A., "The Economics of Happiness." *Daedalus*, Spring 2004.

27  Kahneman, Daniel and Deaton, Angus, "High Income Improves Evaluation of Life but Not Emotional Well-Being." *Psychological and Cognitive Sciences*, September 21, 2010.

28  "Fortune 500 Companies Hold a Record $2.4 Trillion Offshore." Citizens for Tax Justice, March 4, 2016.

29  "Broken at the Top: How America's Dysfunctional Tax System Costs Billions in Corporate Tax Dodging." *Oxfam*, April 14, 2016.

30  "Despite Rising Deficits, IRS Audits of the Largest and Richest Corporations Decline." *TracIRS*, April 12, 2010.

31  "Tax Gap Estimates for Tax Years 2008–2010." Internal Revenue Service, April 2016.

32  Pizzigati, Sam, "Cheating Uncle Sam." *Too Much Online*, October 27, 2008.

33  Henry, James S., "The Price of Offshore Revisited." Tax Justice Network, July 2012.

34  Holtz, Colin, "The Panama Papers Prove It: America Can Afford a Universal Basic Income." *The Guardian*, April 8, 2016.

35  "Global Wealth Databook 2015." Credit Suisse, October 2015.

36  Baker, Dean, "Reining in Wall Street to Benefit All Americans." Center for Economic and Policy Research, July 2016.

37  RobinHoodTax.org.

38  Pollin, Robert and Heintz, James, "The Revenue Potential of a Financial Transaction Tax for U.S. Financial Markets." Political Economy Research Institute, March 9, 2016; Bivens, Josh and Blair, Hunter, "A Financial Transaction Tax Would Help Ensure Wall Street Works for Main Street." Economic Policy Institute, July 28, 2016; Pollin, Robert, "Bernie Sanders Will Make the Economy Great Again." *The Nation*, March 29, 2016.

39  Reich, Robert, "Why Isn't Everyone in Favor of Taxing Financial Speculation?" Commondreams.org, April 19, 2016.

40  Strupczewski, Jan, "Ten EU Countries Agree on Aspects of a Financial-Transaction Tax." Reuters, December 8, 2015.

41  Smithberger, Mandy, "America's $1 Trillion National Security Budget." Project on Government Oversight, February 10, 2016.

42  Engelhardt, Tom, "Tomgram: Engelhardt, Roads to Nowhere, Ghost Soldiers, and a $43 Million Gas Station in Afghanistan." TomDispatch.com, November 12, 2015.

43  Burke, Cathy, "Survey: Most Americans Favor Cutting US Defense Budget." *Newsmax*, March 9, 2016; "Rightsizing Defense: The Perspective of the People." University of Maryland Survey, March 2016.

44  "CPC 'Gang of Six' Releases Framework for Tax Reform." Congressional Progressive Caucus, December 1, 2012; Dungan, Adrian, "Individual Income Tax Shares, 2012." Internal Revenue Service, Spring 2015.

45  Piketty, Thomas; Saez, Emmanuel; Stantcheva, Stefanie: "Taxing the 1%: Why the Top Tax Rate Could be Over 80%." *VOX*, December 2011.

46  Kindermann, Fabian and Krueger, Dirk, "High Marginal Tax Rates on the Top 1%? Lessons from a Life Cycle Model with Idiosyncratic Income Risk." National Bureau of Economic Research, October 2014.

47  Bartlett, Bruce, "What Is the Revenue-Maximizing Tax Rate?" *Tax Analysts*, February 22, 2012.

48  Young, Cristobal; Varner, Charles; Lurie, Ithai; Prisinzano, Richard: "Millionaire Migration and the Taxation of the Elite: Evidence from Administrative Data." Stanford University and U.S. Department of the Treasury, October 20, 2015.

49  Buchheit, Paul, "Tax Avoidance On the Rise: It's Twice the Amount of Social Security and Medicare." Commondreams.org, January 7, 2013; Huang, Chye-Ching and DeBot, Brandon, "Ten Facts You Should Know About the Federal Estate Tax." Center on Budget and Policy Priorities, March 23, 2015; Hill, Steven, "The Sharing Economy will Screw Us All—and It's Retirement We Have to be Really Worried about." *Salon*, May 7, 2016.

50  Piketty, Thomas, *Capital in the Twenty-First Century*. Harvard University Press, 2014.

51  Collins, Chuck and Hoxie, Josh, "Billionaire Bonanza." Institute for Policy Studies, December 1, 2015.

52  Villarreal, Jorge, "To Stop Climate Change, Don't Just Cut Carbon. Redistribute Wealth." Commondreams, August 10, 2016; Biello, David, "How Much Is Too Much?: Estimating Greenhouse Gas Emissions." *Scientific American*, April 29, 2009.

53  George, Henry, *Progress and Poverty*. Appleton & Co., 1879.

54  Reich, Robert, "Labor Day 2028." RobertReich.org, September 1, 2015.

55  Foroohar, Rana, "Why You Can Thank the Government for Your iPhone." *Time*, October 27, 2015.

56 "Federal Low-Income Programs." Government Accountability Office, July 2015
57 Bruenig, Matt, "How a Universal Basic Income Would Affect Poverty." Demos, October 3, 2013.
58 "Agenda of the Just Third Way Movement." Center for Economic and Social Justice, January 19, 2013.
59 "Capital Homestead Act." Center for Economic and Social Justice, 2016.

## Bibliography

Alperovitz, Gar and Daly, Lew, *Unjust Deserts: How the Rich Are Taking Our Common Inheritance and Why We Should Take It Back*. The New Press, 2008.

Bernstein, Jared, *The Reconnection Agenda: Reuniting Growth and Prosperity*. CreateSpace, 2015.

Derber, Charles and Magrass, Yale R., *The Surplus American: How the 1% is Making Us Redundant*. Paradigm, 2012.

George, Henry, *Progress and Poverty*. First Published 1879.

Gordon, Robert J., *The Rise and Fall of American Growth: The U.S. Standard of Living since the Civil War*. Princeton University Press, 2016.

Hanlon, Joseph; Barrientos, Armando; Hulme, David: *Just Give Money to the Poor: The Development Revolution from the Global South*. Kumarian Press, 2010.

Hartmann, Thom, *Rebooting the American Dream: 11 Ways to Rebuild Our Country*. Berrett-Koehler, 2011.

Kaye, Harvey, *Thomas Paine and the Promise of America*. Hill and Wang, 2005.

Klein, Naomi, *This Changes Everything: Capitalism vs. the Climate*. Simon & Schuster, 2014.

Linebaugh, Peter, *Stop, Thief!: The Commons, Enclosures, and Resistance*. PM Press, 2014.

McGoey, Linsey, *No Such Thing as a Free Gift: The Gates Foundation and the Price of Philanthropy*. Verso Books, 2015.

Mazzucato, Mariana, *The Entrepreneurial State: Debunking Public vs. Private Sector Myths*. Anthem Press, 2013.

Piketty, Thomas, *Capital in the Twenty-First Century*. Harvard University Press, 2014.

Susskind, Richard and Susskind, Daniel, *The Future of the Professions: How Technology Will Transform the Work of Human Experts*. Oxford University Press, 2016.

Uchitelle, Louis, *The Disposable American: Layoffs and Their Consequences*. Vintage, 2007.

# INDEX